GREAT HONEYMOON DISASTERS

For Mary with love
and in the hope that this book
will convince her that our honeymoon
was quite long enough.

GREAT HONEYMOON DISASTERS

Simon Welfare
Illustrations by Larry

Arthur Barker Limited London
A subsidiary of Weidenfeld (Publishers) Limited

Published in Great Britain by
Arthur Barker Limited
91 Clapham High Street
London SW4 7TA

ISBN 0 213 16939 8

Printed in Great Britain by
Butler & Tanner Ltd
Frome and London

Acknowledgements

While I was researching this book, I discovered a curious thing. People are always happy to talk about honeymoons, *as long as they don't have to tell you about their own.*

Nothing is more maddening for the diligent gatherer of honeymoon disaster stories than to be told: 'And as for my own honeymoon. Talk about a fiasco! Well, actually, on second thoughts, I'd rather draw a veil over the whole thing.'

So I feel obliged to confess my own honeymoon disaster.

My wife Mary and I spent the first weekend of our married life at the luxurious Gleneagles Hotel in Scotland. Our room was chintzy and comfortable, the barman downstairs mixed heady and exotic cocktails, the food was superb.

We should have known that it was too good to last. On the second evening, disaster struck. (To be honest, I'm not sure to this day that it really *was* a disaster, but my wife is adamant that it was.)

Night was falling over the Highlands; the last trolleys had creaked home from the Gleneagles golf courses, and we dined particularly well.

Too well, as it turned out.

We hadn't a problem in the world, except for one. What were we going to do after dinner? It was too early, even for honeymooners, to retire to bed, and far too cool that summer evening to go roamin' romantically in the gloamin'.

We decided (this was long before the days of in-house video) to go to the hotel film show. It was held in a small room and the rows of chairs were close together.

The film was a comedy, and we laughed a lot as we sat there holding hands. About halfway through the film, however, when the audience was silent, I let out a tiny sigh of contentment - which was followed at once by an enormous burp.

Row upon row of well-coiffed heads turned accusingly towards us. Mary has never forgotten that moment, and I, of course, have never been allowed to.

As to the rest of our honeymoon? Talk about a fiasco! Well, actually, on second thoughts, I'd rather draw a veil over the whole thing . . .

So I am particularly grateful to those few people who have told me about their own honeymoon disasters, as well as those, far more in number, who have told me gleefully of the misfortunes of others. My thanks to Julie Biddle, Liz Brice, Arthur C. Clarke, Peter Costello, Michael Deakin, Peggy Duncan, Sheila Fitzhugh, Tom Forsyth, the Earl of Haddo, Adam Hart-Davis, Melvin Harris, John Jeremy, Tina Leeming, Jeremy Lemmon, Lou Lidderdale, Nick Lord, Huon Mallalieu, David Morgan, Pam Roberts, Karen Wright, and especially to Clive Trist whose tale of a painful honeymoon inspired this book.

Many of the stories have been drawn from published material, and I acknowledge with gratitude the help of the staffs of the Aberdeen University Library and the London Library.

Finally, my thanks to Christopher Logue whose 'True

Stories' column in *Private Eye* has been not only the source of many honeymoon stories, but a reminder of the fact that even when things go disastrously wrong we are sometimes allowed to laugh.

SIMON WELFARE

Before a Victorian wedding, one of the prime duties of the Mother of the Bride was to give her daughter a Little Talk about her forthcoming honeymoon. Most important of all was advice about the wedding night and How To React To The Beastly Things Men Get Up To When They Have Got A Young Woman On Her Own.

In some cases the results were bizarre. One Victorian bridegroom, with admirable sensitivity, is said to have left the nuptial chamber to allow his blushing new wife to get ready for bed. After a suitable interval he returned. His heart leaped for joy, for there she lay, stretched out on the silken sheets, the object of all his desires. Unable to restrain himself any longer, he flung himself eagerly on to the four-poster. But the bride did not stir. In fact she was out cold, drugged to the tips of her toes. Pinned to the pillow was this note: 'Mummy says you should do what you wish.'

Modern mothers give rather different advice to their daughters - or sons. 'Make sure you survive the honeymoon,' they say. 'After that, anything - even married life - is easy.'

There's real wisdom in their words, for few honeymooners seem to avoid disaster of one kind or another. (Queen Victoria was one of those lucky few, perhaps because she insisted that her honeymoon at Windsor should last no more than three days. The nation, she

. . . she was out cold, drugged to the tips of her toes.

explained to Albert, would be quite unable to do without her for any longer. However, one observer, Charles Greville, complained that the wedding night itself had been too short, and that 'this was not the way to provide us with a Prince of Wales'.)

Some honeymoon disasters are more catastrophic than others. From the idyllic island of Réunion, in June 1977, *The Times* reported this tragi-comic tale of the ultimate lover's leap:

> A honeymooning Irishman, Mr Philip Ryan, fell 500 feet to his death in a volcano on this Indian Ocean island on Friday night. A fence he vaulted was not around his holiday cottage but around the volcano.

At least pet-shop owners Sandy and David Ison lived to tell the tale of the chapter of accidents visited upon them during their honeymoon. The trouble began for the Oxfordshire couple as they roared through France in their £8,000 Porsche – a wedding present to each other.

First the car broke down. Repairs set them back £100. Then that night, as they slept in their hotel, the romantic roadster was stolen.

Surely, things couldn't get worse? Of course they could. Sandy Ison's finger suddenly swelled up: she was allergic to her gold wedding ring. And later, as they roller-coastered along mountain roads in Austria, their hired car developed gear trouble.

Back in France, Sandy went down with travel sickness, food poisoning and sunstroke. So home to England they staggered; and in Dover Sandy found her purse containing £100 had been stolen.

But the exhausted couple's troubles were far from over. That night, the telephone woke them at 2 a.m. It was the police, reporting a break-in at the pet shop. David dragged himself out of bed to investigate.

When he got to the shop, he found the culprit was a tiny chinchilla which had escaped from its cage and triggered the burglar alarm.

The false alarm was followed by a real break-in, the couple's holiday photographs went missing, and Sandy Ison, having recovered from her allergy, found her wedding ring was too tight and had to send it back to be altered.

A honeymoon to remember - or to forget as quickly as possible.

One bridegroom hit a more intimate snag on his wedding night. He ended up in court accused of breaking into a contraceptive machine and was fined £25, despite a heart-rending excuse. He told the beak that his bride had refused to let him exercise his conjugal rights without taking precautions. Hence his raid on the rubbers.

'All the shops were closed,' the groom explained, 'and neither of us had any change.'

When Peter and Lucia Eachus set off on honeymoon after their wedding in Manchester, they only had eyes for each other. They might have avoided disaster if they had kept them on the road instead. Ahead lay a honeymoon hotel in South Devon - or so they thought.

It seemed a long drive. After many miles Lucia said: 'Is there a Gretna Green near Torquay?'

Now as anyone not blinded by love knows, there is no Gretna Green near Torquay. Gretna is in Scotland, almost 400 miles from palmy South Devon. The Eachuses had driven the wrong way up the motorway. They finally reached their honeymoon hotel 36 hours late and with an extra 900 miles on the clock.

Said 22-year-old Linda: 'It's all very embarrassing. I was navigating. We stopped for a meal on the M6. Then we drove off on the wrong carriageway and didn't notice we were heading north.'

Some people take honeymoon disasters very seriously – and not just the victims. In 1980 Chicago lawyer Herbert Glieberman announced to the world that 20 percent of divorces can be traced back to the first few days and nights of married life. In fact, it did not matter whether the honeymoon was good or bad, he said.

'If it's wonderful, the magical feeling can't be kept up. And if it's a let-down, the trouble starts right away and it's all downhill from there.'

'Save your money, scrap the honeymoon,' was his unromantic advice to couples about to marry.

Fortunately for this book – if not for many a bride and groom – Mr Glieberman's warning seems to have gone unheeded. According to a recent magazine survey, the honeymoon is still seen as an essential part of the ritual of marriage. Despite a typical cost of £630, and the ever-present prospect of disaster ...

The honeymoon really begins when groom and bride – 'a woman with a fine prospect of happiness behind her', as one cynic put it – leave the reception and at last find themselves alone. But life is seldom as neat as that, and the seeds of some honeymoon disasters are sown long before the Happy Couple can shake the confetti out of their hair and, occasionally, even before they reach the church door.

An Oxfordshire couple, John and Angela Thomas, spent much of their honeymoon trailing after their dog Spike. Just before the marriage ceremony, the playful pooch had swiped – and swallowed – Angela's £40 gold wedding ring.

When asked about the golden gulp by a reporter, the bride said: 'We know the ring's still in his tummy because we've been over him with a metal detector. All we can do is wait for nature to take its course, but we have to follow him everywhere.'

Added Angela: 'I'm thinking of putting him in disposable nappies.'

Naomi Nicely of Greensburg, Pennsylvania, never got to go on honeymoon, but she did get married – just. The wedding ceremony had reached a crucial point when Miss Nicely's intended, Robert Neiderhiser, dropped dead at the altar.

The minister, the Rev. Captain Rag of Fort Palmer Unitarian Mission, later described the sorry scene:

'Mr Neiderhiser fell to the floor as he uttered the binding words, "I do." As I bent over him he whispered, "My God – I do," whereupon he died. The ceremony was over.'

Such was the confusion over her marital status, that Miss Nicely – or was she Mrs Neiderhiser? – had to apply to the local court to declare her an 'official widow'.

Wendy Wilkinson's troubles began when she collapsed at the altar during her wedding and had to be revived. After the ceremony, husband Mike adjourned with his pals to a pub in Banbury (you'll have noticed by now that Oxfordshire is a peculiarly disaster-prone county for honeymooners).

Eventually, Wendy caught up with the boozing bridegroom, but they began to argue when Mike, who had given up smoking, lit up once again. Wendy stormed off.

Much later, at about midnight, Mike wandered home expecting the customary comforts of the wedding night. But Wendy was nowhere to be found. She had sought solace elsewhere – at her sister's.

Joan Fenelon Bellars also fainted at the altar. In her case, just as the ring was being slipped on to her finger by her groom and fellow Londoner Peter Cadwell. Joan was unconscious for twenty minutes, and as if that wasn't bad enough, nothing went right after she'd come round. The choir sang the anthem at the wrong point in the service, the vicar fell ill and had to be replaced by a stand-in, the couple's van, in which they had been planning to go away, turned out to contain a cement mixer, and their honeymoon hotel cancelled their booking because of a fire.

So no one was surprised when the groom announced a change of plan: he and the new Mrs Cadwell would now be spending the fortnight in the garden of their cottage – digging a hole for a septic tank.

In Southampton in 1985, violent passions erupted before a planned double wedding.

A pitched battle broke out among the punk and skinhead guests, and one of the couples ended up in separate cells.

Despite the *fracas*, the other couple went ahead with their half of the wedding and later the bridegroom managed to salvage some cheer from the proceedings.

'We are planning to go for an LSD trip in the park tonight,' he said, 'because it's cheaper than a honeymoon.'

There were similar scenes at the marriage of Miss Bindi Sha to Mr Hakim Nid – this time actually in the temple where the ceremony was taking place. First, Miss Sha smashed a bottle of whisky over the head of Mr Nid's father, fracturing his skull. Then the belligerent bride turned on his sister and butted her in the stomach. Her own parents came off little better – mother was locked into the temple lavatory and father was tied up in a half-nelson by the battling Bindi.

While trying to make a getaway, she crashed her fiancé's car and had to escape the furious families on foot.

Later the bridegroom, wifeless and with his honeymoon plans in ruins, told a reporter: 'This is the first time Bindi has expressed any emotion towards me.'

When the great French writer Victor Hugo married Adèle Foucher in October 1822, a wedding dinner was held in the imposing surroundings of the Paris Hôtel de Ville.

During the dinner, some of the guests noticed that Victor's elder brother, Eugène, was behaving very oddly. They removed him discreetly and discovered that Eugène had gone stark, staring crazy. It turned out that he, like his brother, had long been in love with the bride, and now he was, quite literally, madly jealous.

Fortunately, Victor and Adèle were not told the full facts until the next morning.

So, although Eugène's insanity, from which he never recovered, cast a cloud over the honeymoon, the wedding night itself obviously went well, for baby Léopold Hugo arrived exactly 9 months later.

For some people, the only problems affecting their honeymoon are little ones.

During the wedding of Harry and Dora Vale in Conway, the bride had to take time out to give birth to a baby boy in a nearby pew.

Harry seized the opportunity to pay his bride this compliment: 'It was the first I had heard of it,' he said. 'But Dora is an assistant nurse so she knew exactly what to do. When it was over we carried on with the wedding as if nothing had happened.'

Donna Brady of Chingford, Essex, managed to get married and enjoy the reception before dashing to hospital, where she, too, gave birth.

'By the time I'd cut the cake at the reception in my mum's house I knew something was wrong,' she said.

'My baby daughter was the best wedding present I could have wished for.'

'I was as shocked as the wedding guests must have been,' added the bride who had worn a slinky size 10 dress for the ceremony. 'I thought the pains in my stomach were wedding day nerves.'

. . . the bride had to take time out to give birth to a baby boy in a nearby pew.

You might imagine that people who get married for the second time would know enough to avoid disaster. So pity the poor bridegroom I heard of recently who thought he'd got everything planned to give his new marriage the happiest possible start.

The reception was being held at his home and the bridegroom rang his wine merchant and ordered ten cases of champagne. When the bubbly failed to arrive, he realised something had gone wrong.

The wine merchant was adamant that the cases had been despatched. Then the penny dropped.

The bridegroom had assumed that the wine merchant knew his current address. But in fact the shop's list was out of date.

The 120 bottles had been despatched all right – but to the bridegroom's old address, where his first wife had been only too delighted to take delivery ...

A waitress from Taunton, Somerset, made this complicated confession about her wedding.

'I am bound to admit that I only married Geoff to get out of going to Borstal,' she said. She added that she had been arrested after she 'happened to be near some window-smashing done by a close relative of my mother's'.

Fearing that the magistrate would put her inside, she agreed to the suggestion made by her friend Mr Williams that she should marry a man, whom she had met in a pub.

'I forgot to tell Geoff that I was living with Mr Williams at the time, until his divorce arrived and we could find a home of our own,' said the waitress.

. . . out through the emergency exit into Mr Williams' arms.

'We had the ceremony, and after a shrimp cocktail and steak reception, where I drank the groom's health, I went out through the emergency exit into Mr Williams' arms.'

The bridegroom, reacted angrily to the news. At once he rushed round to the registry office and asked for the marriage to be annulled. When this was refused, he tore off his shirt, shouting:

'I never even had it!'

Another Somerset couple were also aggrieved, for they hadn't expected to have to cool their heels in separate police cells after their wedding.

They had decided to save money on a reception and celebrate their marriage in the pub instead. A good time was had by all, but things began to go wrong when the couple left the bar.

A cab was summoned to take them home, but after the bride and three friends had hopped in, there was no room for the bridegroom.

An argument ensued in which the cabby's spectacles were broken and a policeman's clip-on tie was torn off and thrown into the road.

The court was told that the bride had told the police: 'It was my wedding day and I was happy.'

The newlyweds were fined a total of £70 and the bridegroom was ordered to pay another £18.50 for the cabby's glasses.

Later the rueful bridegroom said: 'Looking back on this wedding with nearly £90 to find in costs and fines we could have afforded that reception. It must have been cheaper.'

A surprise of a different sort momentarily marred the happiness of a couple who married in Dudley in the West Midlands in the summer of 1981.

The marriage service, held before 400 guests, was going smoothly; but when the minister reached the traditional challenge 'If anyone knows of any reason why they may not lawfully marry, let him now declare it,' a woman appeared from the back of church and announced: 'Yes, I do.' What's more, she was not alone, for in each arm she held a baby.

The bride and groom, of course, were aghast. Who was this person, and what was she doing interrupting the service? Fortunately, the minister was having none of it. He told the woman that since a certificate for the marriage to take place had already been issued, her protest was not a legal objection. Whereupon the woman promptly left the church, taking her babies with her. By the time anyone thought to ask her to explain her actions, she was gone.

That this turned out to be no more than a near-honeymoon-disaster is thanks to the wise and plucky attitude of the astonished newlyweds. Said the bride later: 'We did not let it spoil our day.'

All too often, when the euphoria of the wedding party and the champagne have worn off, a honeymoon turns out to be a time for regrets. That much-married Hollywood star Eva Gabor probably holds the record for speedy second thoughts.

Describing her marriage to her third husband, a Beverly Hills plastic surgeon called John Williams, Eva confided to a columnist: 'I wasn't in love with him. I didn't even like him. And after we were married for one minute, I wanted to leave him.'

Italian bride Marisa Carlotta took a little longer to see the error of her ways – a matter of three hours.

At the reception after her marriage to Giuseppe Moretti in Rome, Marisa met an old boyfriend, a childhood sweetheart who had emigrated to America but had returned for the wedding.

They exchanged glances. They talked. Old flames were rekindled. At once they decided that they still loved each other, and, without further ado, left immediately for the airport and caught a plane to New York.

The composer Tchaikovsky was a little more chivalrous towards his new wife, whom he married in July 1877. He didn't allow regrets to assail him until he and his bride were in the train on their way to honeymoon in St Petersburg. But he then really made up for lost time.

A bare two days after the wedding, Tchaikovsky wrote to his brother: 'When the train started I was ready to scream; sobs choked me.' He described his wedding as 'ghastly spiritual torture' and his wife as 'very limited'.

The problem was that poor old Tchaikovsky suffered from 'an abnormal disposition', as one of his biographers wrote in the days when closets were to hang clothes in and not to come out of.

In the circumstances it is amazing the marriage lasted as long as it did: nine weeks, including the honeymoon.

Regrets also quickly overcame the New Zealand-born writer Katherine Mansfield after her marriage to musician George Bowden in 1909. That same evening, she upped and fled from their honeymoon hotel. One reason put forward to explain the bridal bolt is that Katherine simply took against the décor of her room.

There is nothing like a row for inspiring second thoughts. Sir Richard Blake and Bertice Reading made an unlikely couple when they married in Chichester Cathedral. He was a baronet from an old Irish family; she was a roly-poly jazz singer and nine years older than her groom. When Sir Richard filed for divorce three years later, Bertice told a reporter that things had begun to go wrong when she and her husband quarrelled during a celebration dinner after the wedding.

'He told me,' said Bertice, '"Today I have given you a great gift – I have made you a lady." I said, "I was a lady before you were even born." He really upset me, so I took my flowers and left.'

Sir Richard had different memories and denied insulting his bride.

'She didn't even spend the wedding night with me,' he said. 'She went off within a few days to make a film; then she went bankrupt, which I didn't know anything about.'

American heiress Barbara Hutton began to realise her mistake as her luxurious honeymoon train swept through the night towards her romantic Italian villa. It was time to slip into something loose. From her fabulous trousseau, packed into thirteen suitcases, the buxom Barbara chose an elegant silk nightgown. Meanwhile, husband Prince Alexis Mdivani sat at the end of the bed, staring and silent, apparently rapt with lust and love. Finally he spoke.

'Barbara,' he said, 'you are too fat.'

The Swedish dramatist August Strindberg must have given his second wife pause for thought on their wedding night. Strindberg, in fact, was a gloomy fellow who, although he married three times, never seems to have got along with women. Certainly all his marriages came bitterly to grief.

During their wedding night in Heligoland, Strindberg's second wife suddenly awoke to find her husband's hands around her neck. But this was no fond caress: he was trying to strangle her in his sleep! Mrs Strindberg fought for her life and, after a furious struggle, finally broke free.

It was only then that Strindberg himself came to; and, as his wife sat shocked and gasping at his side, he courteously explained that he had no murderous intentions towards her. He had simply thought, half asleep, that she was his first wife, and (old fantasies die hard) had naturally wanted to kill her.

King George IV took a dislike to his wife, Caroline of Brunswick, as soon as he saw her. In fact, 'dislike' is too mild a word, for the horrified monarch retreated to the far end of the room and whispered to the Earl of

Malmesbury, 'Harris, I am not well, pray get me a glass of brandy.'

But the marriage went through, and on the wedding night in 1795 the sulking sovereign's regrets grew more intense. He arrived in the bedroom well fortified with brandy. The marriage was quickly consummated (Caroline gave birth to a daughter exactly nine months later) and the King spent the rest of his wedding night sprawled in the fireplace, snoring his head off.

What put Prinny off? After almost two centuries of speculation, honeymoon historians have come up with no definite answer, but there's an unsavoury probability that Caroline simply stank on her wedding night. Her disregard for personal hygiene was legendary - when she first reached England, for example, she is said to have refused to have a bath, on the grounds that she had already had one in Germany!

Was Ingeborg of Denmark another revolting royal? In the twelfth century she married King Philip Augustus of France. Their honeymoon - and their marriage - lasted only one night. In the morning, the king put her away for ever. Exactly what happened is a mystery which - perhaps like Ingeborg - remains impenetrable.

Ingeborg must have discovered what many others have later learned: if there's one time when any honeymoon is particularly prone to disaster, it is on the morning after the wedding night.

For poet and critic Al Alvarez the moment of truth came when he took breakfast to his sleeping bride. He describes the scene in his book *Life After Marriage*:

I poured tea. 'It's a lovely morning,' I said. Her silence was making me nervous.

She bit into her toast, then put it down in dismay. Her first words that morning were 'You didn't cut off the crusts.'

The marriage was doomed.

Insurance broker Ken Simkin also had regrets on the day after, but, he told an American court, he hadn't exactly gone into marriage with his eyes open.

One morning, after a booze-up, Ken awoke and found himself in bed with an 18-stone blonde called 'Big Mama'.

'It was like waking up next to a sperm whale,' he said. 'But, through my hangover, it began to dawn on me that I'd married her. It was a terrible feeling.'

Ken claimed 'Big Mama' had made off with his 30 ft yacht and thousands of dollars in cash. Yet he agreed that even this connubial cloud had a silver lining:

'One good thing's come out of this,' he said. 'I was drinking a lot once – but haven't been drunk since that awful morning.'

A recent Gallup Poll listed the little habits that make marriages less than perfect. The wives couldn't stand the

... Ken awoke and found himself in bed with an 18-stone blonde ...

way their men left toenail cuttings on the floor or went to bed with their socks on.

The men complained about being nagged to check things in the house, and were positively exasperated by women who could not find fifth gear in a car.

Such irritating quirks of character and behaviour tend not to appear until the honeymoon. It is then that many a bride and groom have made amazing – and sometimes unwelcome – discoveries about each other.

The great British actor Charles Laughton put it in a nutshell. He was once asked whether he would ever consider marrying again. The question was hypothetical, for Laughton was already married. To the questioner's surprise, Laughton replied that nothing would induce him to consider matrimony again.

When pressed for his reasons, Laughton explained: 'During courtship a man reveals only his better qualities. After marriage, however, his real self gradually begins to emerge and there is very little his wife can do about it. I don't believe I would ever put a woman through that again.'

Women, of course, also reveal their true selves on honeymoon. A Suffolk man, Mr A. R. Mahler – perhaps rather ungallantly – came up with this example in a letter to a newspaper which had asked its readers to describe their most spine-chilling moment:

> My most spine-chilling moment was seeing my new bride wearing a face-pack for the first time. I went white to match.

And in another letter to a paper, a Mrs Doyle of London described the shocking scene that met her eyes on the morning after her wedding as she entered the bedroom with a cup of tea for her husband:

> As I took it into our lovely new pale green and white bedroom, I screamed with horror.
>
> There he was, cleaning his black shoes in bed!
>
> 'Don't worry love,' he said. 'I've done it all my life. You won't find any black marks.'

And, as any new husband should be, the bedroom boot-black was true to his word: not a single smudge of polish appeared on the bedclothes in the twenty-five years that followed.

Sir Edward Marshall Hall, the great English lawyer who featured in many of the sensational trials of the nineteenth and twentieth centuries, made a most unfortunate discovery about his bride, Ethel, while they were driving away from the church after their wedding in 1882.

As they sat together in the carriage, Ethel announced that she had never cared for him and saw no prospect of ever being able to do so. This was something of a problem for Hall, and despite his skills as an advocate, he was quite unable to win her round. The honeymoon in Paris was of course a nightmare, and when they returned to England the lovesick lawyer understandably sought consolation in some mildly murderous pursuits – such as shooting the pike in the pond at his sister's house and bagging bats with his shotgun.

Although Marshall Hall for the most part managed to keep a stiff upper lip about his troubles, most marriage break-ups bring recriminations in their wake.

My favourite case was reported in 1982. A woman from Bradford, Yorkshire, had married a man she had met through a pensioners' pen-pal service. Romance had quickly blossomed, and soon the letter-writing lovebirds were wed. But, according to the bride, she quickly realised that 'it was all a terrible mistake'.

So what had gone wrong? The bride gave two reasons to a journalist. The first was familiar in such cases: her husband, she claimed, had been too jealous and hadn't liked it if anyone spoke to her. The second was, to say the least, less common. The husband had apparently not been entirely frank about his age. He turned out to be 89, but 'He said he was only 83,' the bride complained.

That notably unsensitive soul, King Ferdinand IV of the Two Sicilies, when asked about his new bride on the morning after his wedding night replied: 'Suda come un porco' – 'She sweats like a pig.'

Catherine the Great of Russia discovered that her bridegroom preferred playing with toy soldiers on the bedcover to more macho manoeuvres beneath it.

Most famously of all, the nineteenth-century art critic John Ruskin was shocked – alas, far from rigid – when he first saw his new wife Effie undressed after their marriage in 1848. She was, he told her cryptically, 'quite different' from what he had imagined nude women to look like.

. . . her bridegroom preferred playing with toy soldiers on the bedcover to more macho manoeuvres beneath it.

Indeed, the shock of first seeing their spouse undressed seems to have been too much for many Victorians.

Charles Kingsley, author of *The Water Babies*, gave the matter a great deal of thought before his marriage to Fanny Grenfell in 1844.

'I have been thinking over your terror at seeing me undressed,' he wrote to Fanny, 'and I feel that I should have the same feeling in a minor degree to you, till I had learnt to bear the blaze of your naked beauty. You do not know how often a man is struck powerless in body and mind on his wedding night.'

Kingsley's plan was that they should take things slowly. And so they did. For the first month of their five week honeymoon near Cheddar, the Kingsleys abstained from sex. In the fifth week, they reportedly made up for lost time with great enthusiasm and consummated the marriage.

Austrian Civil Servant Werner Seitenbaum, on the other hand, spent a conventional wedding night with his bride Anita. His shock discovery came after several months of marriage.

The couple had scrimped and saved for a belated honeymoon – on safari in Kenya. The first fortnight of the trip was idyllic. The happy couple spent their days photographing exotic wildlife in game parks; at night they dined on gourmet cuisine and danced cheek-to-cheek in the velvet African night.

But in the third week, a change seemed to come over the bridegroom. Werner had suddenly lost his exuberant energy. He even felt too tired and listless to dance in the discotheque. The only thing for it was to go to bed early, and apologetically he bade his bride goodnight.

Werner slept through until almost noon, but that evening, he felt no better. After a couple of drinks he was exhausted. And it was the same the night after that, and the night after that . . .

On the last night, however, Werner, who had once again gone to bed early, awoke at 1.30 a.m. and realised his wife was not lying beside him. Nor, he established after a quick search, was she anywhere near their honeymoon bungalow.

So a worried Werner settled down to wait. At last, just before dawn, Frau Seitenbaum crept through the bedroom and went straight into the bathroom.

The distraught husband flung open the door. There, in front of the mirror, sat his wife taking off her make-up. But what make-up! Her face was daubed with African tribal paint.

A furious row ensued. Werner slapped his wife and left for the airport. The honeymoon was over and so was the marriage.

Later, at the divorce court, Anita explained. The honeymoon had, indeed, begun blissfully. The photographic safaris, the dancing and the African nights had all been wonderful. But best of all was the hotel cabaret, and most beautiful of all a long-limbed dancer named Jonas.

'He was a superb specimen,' she confessed, 'and I was completely infatuated with him.'

So she'd laced her husband's drinks with sleeping pills, and, every night, with Werner fast asleep, she'd sallied forth on a sexy safari.

Werner would have been none the wiser, if it hadn't been for his Civil Servant's caution. On the last night of the honeymoon, he'd decided to have no drinks at all to ensure he'd be fresh for the journey home.

'If it hadn't been for that,' he said, 'Anita would still be my wife and we both would have been remembering Africa for entirely different reasons.'

One of the most bizarre stories of honeymoon discovery that I have come across appears in a book by Brad Steiger, a leading American collector of reported psychic phenomena.

Apparently a widower took a second wife. Everything was fine except for one thing: the bride kept waking up suddenly in the night to find a cold and ghostly hand around her neck trying to squeeze the very life out of her.

Every time this happened, she would try to rouse her husband. But he simply slept on. The strange thing was that he would always mutter the same sentence: 'It's in the black box.'

Soon the bride was a bundle of nerves. Her mother was called in to soothe her.

Then, one day, mother had an idea. She took her distraught daughter up to the loft, and there they found a black box. Could this be the one the husband had been muttering about in his sleep? With trembling hands they opened the lid, and saw inside a tiny urn. The penny dropped.

'His dead wife's ashes!' they cried in chorus.

And so they were. Had the first wife been trying to get her husband to bury her remains and were the attempts at murder signs of jealousy from beyond the grave? That was the second wife's theory, as she paused briefly to ponder the spectral saga – on her way to the divorce court.

The strange fate that befell Mr Robert Michaels of Exeter on his honeymoon was reported by the *Southern Evening Echo:*

> I admit I married my wife because she was a weightlifter and after we had enjoyed ourselves she said she would beat me up unless I became her husband, but I received a profound shock when I discovered that she was also a prostitute.
>
> Two days after we were married I came home after drawing my social security and found the house full of Hell's Angels.
>
> My wife told me to wait in the kitchen until she had finished work. After a few minutes she came into the kitchen in tears. She said that one of the Hell's Angels had left the house in disgust as soon as she took her clothes off. When I tried to cheer her up she turned nasty and insisted that I become a prostitute too.
>
> It took me weeks to get into the job. But the charge that I am living off my wife's immoral earnings is quite untrue. We pool what we earn. It comes to about £9 a week, plus the security, and this is not enough to satisfy her longing for expensive clothes.
>
> We are both very unhappy, but we have decided to make a go of it.

The new bride of one-legged American Tom Porter was convinced she was his 'one and only' – until she found him in bed with another woman.

A row erupted, in which Tom's crutch went flying, a window was broken, and the amorous amputee was carted off to court in Fort Wayne, Indiana.

There, Tom's lawyer broke the news. He told the

judge that the bride had been bamboozled: his client already had two other bigamous wives.

'Hell, that's nothing!' interrupted the truculent Tom. 'I've got three more in Alabama!'

A year or two ago, the honeymoon of a couple from Michigan in the U.S.A. was blighted by the publication of their wedding photo in the local paper.

It was an unusual match – the bride was 83 and her groom 24 – but all went well until the nineteenth day.

Said the bride: 'We attended to each other like young lovebirds.'

That was until the sheriff called and announced that the bridegroom was on the run from the local penitentiary. So the escapee was duly hauled off to the slammer to complete his sentence, leaving the bride to be consoled by her daughter, aged 67, and her grandson who was a mere decade older than her new husband.

A Mr Robinson's local paper in Bedford blew his guilty secret.

The paper published his wedding photo where it was spotted by Mr James Fripp, a tailor and a man with an eagle eye for the cut of a suit.

Mr Fripp looked at the picture closely, and then even more closely, for he recognised Mr Robinson's rigout. He had hired it to Mr Robinson seven years earlier for £6.50 and hadn't seen it since.

After his arrest, Mr Robinson gave this reason for wearing the suit to his wedding: 'I just threw it on at the last minute,' he said, 'because I was in a hurry to get away.'

Honeymoons, of course, really have only one purpose: sex. Even in this permissive age, many girls – and, indeed, boys – manage to 'save themselves' until the wedding night. I'm particularly fond of this justification for remaining a virgin until marriage. It comes from a famous American Christian rock singer. After her wedding in 1982 she told her husband:

> Man that was tough. There were a lot of guys I loved deeply and could have enjoyed knowing fully – man to woman, woman to man. But I persevered so that I could give myself to you.

Good for her, but some people don't realise that it is advisable to use the wait to find out exactly what to do and how to do it. Otherwise, embarrassment, if not disaster, is likely to follow.

In *Goodbye To All That*, writer Robert Graves's brief account of the night that followed his World War I wedding says it all:

> The embarrassments of our wedding night (Nancy and I being both virgins) were somewhat eased by an air raid: Zeppelin bombs dropping not far off set the hotel in an uproar.

The embarrassments of our wedding night . . .

An Indian girl living in Britain was more explicit in a recent newspaper feature. When she married, she was ignorant of the facts of life - like any well-brought-up girl from her culture. She assumed her husband, who was four years older, would know what to do. But no one had told him either, and he had been too shy to ask.

Luckily, the innocent couple were spending their wedding night at the bride's home, and at midnight she was knocking nervously on the door of her parents' bedroom, hoping for some timely advice ...

I imagine that American anthropologist Margaret Mead knew the facts when she married her first husband, Luther Cressman, in 1923, but translating that knowledge into action was something else.

The couple spent their honeymoon in a cottage at Hyannis on Cape Cod. Curiously, the bride, who was 21, insisted upon a separate bedroom, because she had some work to do. Yet that wasn't the problem. She was by no means reluctant; it was simply that, as Cressman later recalled, 'there was nothing doing' on the first two nights.

But on the third day of the honeymoon, 'she got very eager to fondle me while I was driving and I had to tell her, "Watch what you're doing, or we'll end up in a ditch!"'

Happily, they ended up in bed, and Cressman and the avid anthropologist finally consummated their union before dinner.

Our ancestors made no bones about it. They knew what honeymoons were for. Not for them the sniggers as the bride and groom leave the reception or the statutory smutty jokes of the best man's speech. They used to escort the newlyweds to their bedroom and made sure they were tucked up together ready for action. Often, according to Lawrence Wright who wrote an entertaining history of beds and the strange things people have got up to therein, the wedding guests sang naughty songs outside the door to remind the couple of what was expected of them. Wright also tells of how disaster occasionally overtook the revellers:

> At Gilbert White's village of Selborne they recall the accident on the wedding night of one of the older inhabitants, still flourishing there, whose brass double bed was broken amidships by the weight of the guests, so that it had to be carried down the street to the blacksmith, welded together, and brought back amid cheers in time for the climax of the ceremony.

Charles II obviously enjoyed such rituals to the full. When William of Orange married Mary in 1677, the merry monarch led them to the bridal bed crying 'Now, nephew, to your work! Hey, St George for England!'

Such customs died out in the more prudish nineteenth century, but today's honeymooners seem to find plenty to distract them from their duties.

History does not record exactly what it was that caused German car salesman Klaus Lang's failure to 'rise to the occasion' (as one reporter of this extraordinary story delicately described it), but the consequences were comic and almost calamitous.

Leaving his bride unsatisfied, Klaus slunk out of the

bedroom to the nearest bar, there to drown his sorrows. In this, at least, he was successful, and he finally fell into a drunken stupor in a bus shelter.

By one of those strange coincidences that fortunately tend to occur in this kind of story, a party of Klaus's friends chanced to be passing by on a coach trip. They were a good hundred miles from home and well into a thorough survey of the local watering-holes.

When the revellers saw the comatose Klaus they assumed that he, too, was on the outing and bundled him into their bus. On reaching home, they took him to his flat, undressed him and put him to bed with all the tender loving care that drunks have for each other.

Next morning, when Klaus awoke in his flat in Bonn, the full horror of what had happened gradually dawned on him through a monumental hangover.

'I opened my eyes on my honeymoon morning,' he said, 'and found myself back at home - alone. I thought she'd divorce me for sure. Not only do I let her down in bed, but I leave her alone on the wedding night.'

Meanwhile, back at the honeymoon hotel in Cochem, a distraught Frau Rita Lang had alerted the police. Just as they were preparing to drag the nearby river, Klaus telephoned to beg forgiveness.

After that, events moved quickly.

Rita forgave Klaus.

Klaus returned from Bonn.

Rita and Klaus went back to bed.

This time, Klaus got it right on the night.

There was no such happy ending, however, to the honeymoon of a London widower and his bride. The husband was recently granted a divorce because of his wife's inability to consummate their marriage.

At the time of the divorce the bride was 24 and her husband 92.

A forgetful historian told me the following story. She can remember neither the names of the people involved nor the place where this sorry saga unfolded, but she is certain the main facts are true ...

Apparently a German Crown Prince got married and court bureaucrats chose a suitably remote castle for the honeymoon. Stiff Teutonic protocol, however, ensured that two officials each believed that the duty of conveying instructions to the chatelaine belonged to the other.

So when the young bride and bridegroom arrived no one was expecting them and no arrangements had been made. No food had been prepared, the state rooms were under dustsheets and the bed had not been aired.

The chatelaine was distraught, but the place was soon made habitable and the couple repaired to the bedroom.

The officials, however, had overlooked one crucial thing. The wretched prince, though over sixteen, had shown no signs of puberty at all, and that, on the night, must have been the greatest disaster of them all ...

Napoleon Bonaparte certainly had no potency problems on his wedding night. In fact, when he and the legendary Josephine got to bed, they were soon happily and vigorously making love. But suddenly the Emperor let out a bloodcurdling yell – and not out of ecstasy. At the height of the action, Josephine's pet poodle, Fortuné, thinking

. . . had leapt onto the bed and sunk his teeth into the imperial left calf.

his mistress was being attacked, had leapt on to the bed and sunk his teeth into the imperial left calf. The incident led to one of the strangest wedding night ultimata on record. When Napoleon tried to banish the pernicious poodle from the bedroom, Josephine is said to have declared (roughly translated): 'If you want to canoodle, you must put up with my poodle!'

Ian and Anne Marie Coombe of Glasgow were also hounded on honeymoon. Their wedding went smoothly and happily, and for Anne Marie the day had only one worry. Shep, the black-and-white collie she had had since childhood, had gone missing that morning.

So after the reception Anne Marie persuaded Ian to go back to her family home to see if Shep had turned up. He had, and, since the house was locked up, the honeymooners took him back to their flat.

'Everything was fine', Anne Marie wrote later, 'until we went to bed. As Ian began to put his arm around me, Shep went mad and leapt on the bed between us.

'Ian thought he was kidding until Shep gave a ferocious growl, showed his teeth and prepared to pounce.

'Every time Ian tried to touch me, Shep grew nastier. And the more I tried to calm Shep down, the worse he got.

'In the end we gave up – with Ian still pinned to the wall and me having one of the quietest honeymoon nights on record.'

An American magazine, the *Sun*, featured Shirley Barthorpe's account of her weird wedding night. Shirley had married Roy, a bus driver and a widower.

'Almost from the moment we walked into Roy's house and began unpacking, strange things began to happen.

'First, a dog began howling right outside our bedroom window. I threw a shoe at it, but it refused to move.

'Then, just as I was slipping into a sexy negligée, a plate crashed from the wall and shattered.

'I was a nervous wreck, but I took a glass of champagne and settled down. Then a leg fell off the bed. Have you ever tried to lie on a bed with three quarters up and one down?'

Then, Shirley says, she suddenly heard a woman laughing and saw a ghostly but all too familiar figure darting about the room.

'I recognised her as his deceased wife from photos Roy showed me. It was obvious the woman was mad with jealousy and was playing tricks on us. But I was determined to stick it through – until the dressing table collapsed beneath the weight of our wedding presents.

'That was the last straw. I told Roy, "She doesn't intend to let us get on with this. Goodnight and goodbye." I left the house, baggage and wedding gown in hand.'

An Essex couple, Robin and Maria Evans, spent their wedding night at the house of Maria's mother. They had to share a single bed, but such things are no problem when you're young and in love . . . Said Maria:

'While getting down to the nitty-gritty there was a knock at the door. It was one drunk brother-in-law.

'Then came another knock and another drunk brother-in-law, followed by the family, one by one. This continued until 4.30 in the morning.

'My husband was then so tired he fell asleep.'

For Mr and Mrs Arthur Millbank, the flames of love were apparently all too real. The trouble began when Mrs Millbank noticed that the mattress upon which they were consummating their marriage was on fire.

Arthur seized the mattress and dumped it in the back garden.

The couple sank gratefully back on to the bed. Even bare bedsprings could not dull their ardour. But their bouncing bliss was short-lived, for suddenly into the room burst the fire brigade. It turned out that the neighbours had summoned them to put out a fire in their fence – started by the burning mattress. Needless to say, all passion was also temporarily extinguished.

After that, you'll probably be glad to hear that firemen themselves are not immune to disturbed wedding nights. A Devonshire man, Peter Stevens, went to bed with his bride – and his bleeper.

As he slid between the sheets, the bleeper went off. Out jumped Peter and raced to the scene of a £500,000 blaze.

So did his marriage, too, go up in smoke? Not at all. Said his understanding bride Debbie:

'Just because we're married you can't expect Peter to give it up. I expected him to go.'

The poet Shelley's wedding night with Harriet Westbrook in 1811 was not exactly a lyrical experience either, thanks to an interruption from the landlord of the Edinburgh inn where they began their honeymoon.

Shelley answered a knock at the door, only to find the landlord leering outside. Said the innkeeper:

. . . suddenly into the room burst the fire brigade.

'It is customary here at weddings for the guests to come in, in the middle of the night, and wash the bride with whisky.'

Obviously the plan had to be, well, scotched, and, seizing a brace of pistols, the pugnacious poet cried: 'I have had enough of your impertinence; if you give me any more of it I will blow your brains out!'

Thereby so terrifying the landlord that he fell down the stairs.

The last thing one anonymous writer, sheltering under the initials A.T., wanted on her wedding night was to be saved by the bell. Here's the blow-by-blow account Mrs A. T. of Castleford, West Yorkshire, gave in a letter to a national newspaper:

> Foolishly, we honeymooned at my invalid mother-in-law's house.
>
> She keeps a little bell in her bedroom to call for help. So our love match was more like a boxing match on our first night. Always at the wrong moments, she gonged us 13 times!

Most newlyweds, if they can afford to do so – or even if they can't – choose to spend the first few days of married life in an hotel. The Americans and Japanese, as you might expect, offer couples specially designed honeymoon hideaways, complete with heart-shaped bathtubs, revolving beds and stimulating videos. I found this 'Advice to Honeymooners about to Start on a Continental Trip' in an old copy of *Punch*:

> The most appropriate place for *les noces* should be 'The Hotel Marry-time, Calais.'

And while we're on the subject of groanworthy honeymoon jokes from Mr Punch, how about this one:

> *Married Sister*: And of course, Laura, you will go to Rome or Florence for your honeymoon?
> *Laura*: Oh dear, no! I couldn't think of going further than the Isle of Wight with a man I know little or nothing of!

But whatever establishment they choose, no matter in what part of the world, honeymooners seem to become particularly disaster-prone once they've entered the portals of an hotel. For some unlucky souls, embarrassment and mayhem seem to lurk behind every potted palm and bedroom door . . .

A Birmingham woman recently wrote to a newspaper and described how her wedding night in a posh hotel went 'on air':

> We turned off the lights and radio on the bed headboard and were soon giggling and lovey-dovey. Until a voice boomed: 'Can I help you?' Accidentally we had switched on the hotel intercom.

Audrey Letton's hotel hitch produced a touching cry from the heart. Audrey and her husband John had booked their honeymoon at a Welsh hotel well in advance. But when they reached their room they found not the vast double bed they were expecting for their first night frolics, but two single ones. What's more, the beds were on opposite sides of the room and faced in different directions.

It was all too much for 36-year-old Audrey. She took herself and her new husband back home to a full-sized double bed, leaving the hotel manager in no doubt as to the reason for her fury: 'I can't wait,' she cried. 'I've been saving myself.'

Patrick Heffernan had a very happy wedding day. Too happy, in fact, as his bride Tracy-Ann realised when they reached the bridal suite. What Tracy-Ann didn't know, as the jovial Patrick staggered dizzily over the threshold, was that her new husband had been knocking back whiskies with his brother at the reception.

'When we went up to our hotel room,' said Tracy-Ann, 'he tripped a few times, but I put it down to first-night nerves. He walked into the room and I locked the door. When I turned round he had passed out cold beside the bed.'

Tenderly, Tracy-Ann lifted her husband on to the bed and undressed him. There was no need to wake him – after all a lifetime of loving stretched before them – and there was always the morning. Patrick slept on, and soon the weary bride was nodding off.

But things might have been different, had Tracy-Ann remembered the hotel rules in time.

'He woke at 11.30 next morning,' she later recalled,

'but we had to be out of our room by noon, so we didn't even have time for a cuddle.'

Writer Patricia Francis is clearly a fellow-connoisseur of honeymoon disasters. Her own experience of the first fortnight of wedded bliss in Italy inspired her to ask her friends for their stories, which she published to hilarious effect in *Annabel* magazine.

Patricia herself managed to confuse anti-diarrhoea pills with travel sickness tablets. So she and her husband took the anti-tummy-bug pills on the plane and the travel sickness ones three times a day. Now the trouble with travel sickness pills is that they can make you feel very sleepy, so the couple's first few days of married life were plagued with tiredness - and Montezuma's revenge!

Patricia's two best stories about other people's honeymoons both took place in hotels. The first concerns a couple who booked into an hotel in London. After dinner on their wedding night, they duly picked up their key from the night porter and went up to their room.

Ten minutes later, when neither bride nor groom were in a position to receive visitors, there was a loud knocking at the door. It was the night porter and he seemed determined to get in.

The bride rushed to the door and managed to keep the porter from entering the room, while her husband boldly told the would-be intruder to 'Get out'.

At last the porter gave up. Angrily, the bridegroom telephoned Reception to demand an explanation. It turned out that he had thriftily taken advantage of a 'two for the price of one offer' and had rented the room at a bargain rate. The problem was that nobody had told the porter about the arrangement, and he had assumed the young man had smuggled a girlfriend up to his room for a bit of free hanky-panky.

Another of Patricia Francis's friends spent her honeymoon in an idyllic hotel in the Austrian Tyrol. She and her new husband arrived there in the middle of the day, weary and travel-stained. So she decided to freshen up by having a bath.

The hotel was not one of those plastic and concrete dormitories with all mod cons that holidaymakers usually choose, so guests had to share a bathroom. The bride didn't mind at all, and she slipped gratefully out of her going-away outfit and trotted discreetly down the corridor to have a restorative shower.

Afterwards, wrapped only in a bath towel, she went back to the bedroom. But the door was locked. She knocked on it, for she knew her husband was inside. There was no reply. She knocked again – and again – and again. There was silence save for the sound of sheep-bells in the distance and the murmer of conversation from the lunchtime guests in the restaurant below. She shouted, she kicked, she screamed, but all to no avail.

There was nothing for it but to get help. So downstairs she went, still clad in nothing but the Tyrolean towel, past rows of ogling regulars, to ask for the pass-key. And dozens of eyes feasted upon her blushing person as she came back with the manageress.

The pass-key of course did the trick. The bedroom door sprang open, and there on the bed lay the bridegroom, snoring his head off, oblivious to the little drama that had been played out around him.

My friend Arthur C. Clarke (himself no stranger to honeymoon disasters – his luggage and that of his bride was lost by a New York hotel) remembers reading a story about a man who dedicated his life to a search for the Great Sea Serpent of mariners' yarns. Despite his obsession, the hunter managed to find time to fall in love and get married.

He and his wife set off on their honeymoon journey, by sea of course. But, as they stood hand in hand on the deck of their loveboat on their wedding evening, huge serpentine coils loomed up from the deep. From that moment, the monster-hunter lost interest in his bride and never gave her another thought . . .

Now I've never heard of a honeymooner spotting a sea monster in real life, and anyway, providing he or she had a camera or a huge net about their person, such an encounter would hardly be a disaster. But people do get into some decidedly curious situations in the first few days and weeks of married life.

Strangest of all, perhaps, is the story of Diane de Poitiers, mistress of King Henry II of France in the 16th century. On her wedding night, the delicious Diane found herself being pursued round the bedroom not by a lustful husband but by that rare and sometimes dangerous atmospheric phenomenon ball lightning.

. . . From that moment, the monster-hunter lost interest in his bride . . .

Consider the case, too, of a certain Lord Charles Beresford who married at the beginning of this century. On his wedding night, in an excess of enthusiasm and intent on surprising and delighting his loved one, the boisterous Beresford is said to have burst into her bedroom and flung himself upon his bride's white body with merry cries of 'Cock-a-doodle-do!'

Only to find himself in bed between the Bishop of Chester and his lady wife.

A bridegroom from Wiltshire made a rather similar mistake – but he ended up in jail.

He and his bride were honeymooning in Crete. One night, after a few drinks in the hotel bar, the bride decided to go up to bed. But her husband didn't feel tired and went for a stroll.

It was when he tried to get back into the hotel that he made his fatal blunder. To his surprise he couldn't get in. So he used a little force. A window was smashed. There were screams and the lights flashed on. Soon afterwards, the police arrived. Only then did the bridegroom discover that he had mistaken a private house for his honeymoon hotel.

A far worse discovery came later. The Cretan authorities are not sympathetic to honeymoon disasters, and the bridegroom was thrown into prison, sentenced to eleven months.

An American in London also ended up on the wrong side of the law. Right from the start of his honeymoon, nothing went right for the unfortunate man. First he was conned into shelling out £20 a week for a 'holiday flat' which turned out to be a squat. Then he was caught shoplifting and fined £50.

For the bride, this was the last straw, and, the groom claimed, she decamped with all that was left of his cash. He had set out from Kansas City with £3,000 in his wallet. Now he had only 80 pence to his name, and no bride.

It was time for desperate measures – or so thought the grief-stricken groom. What did he do to try to persuade his bride to return to him? He went shoplifting again, and ended up in the dock once more.

'I thought it would induce her to come back,' the forsaken bridegroom told the magistrate. But no one was sympathetic, neither beak nor bride, and the luckless American, unable to pay yet another fine, was consigned to that unsought-for destination of many an errant honeymooner – the cells.

And while we're on the subject of crime, it would be hard to beat the plea in mitigation advanced by Rodney Parker's lawyer. Rodney had been pulled out of bed on honeymoon and arrested. Said his solicitor: 'Mr Parker did not flee to Newcastle to escape justice, but to enjoy his honeymoon.'

Paul and Gillian Farrimond of Chorley, Lancashire, suffered a rude awakening of a different kind. They had set up home across the road from the town fire station.

On the morning after they had returned home from the first part of their honeymoon trip, they were awoken from their slumbers by this message blaring forth from the fire station's loudspeakers:

'GOOD MORNING! WE HOPE YOU'VE HAD A GOOD NIGHT'S REST!'

And who had put the firemen up to this merry prank? Why, none other than Paul's auntie who had written to the helmeted heroes:

'I would greatly appreciate it if you could all tiptoe in and out and push your engine down the road, as he needs all the rest he can get, poor lad!'

Mike Cox wasn't allowed a lie-in either on his morning-after-the-night-before. He was dragged out of bed and the arms of his bride Michelle to play football.

He hadn't, of course, been slated to play that morning, but most of his team-mates were too pie-eyed to shoot straight after the reception the previous evening.

Despite the defections, Mike's team, Henbury, thrashed their rivals, St Joseph's, 2–0, with one of the goals put away by the bridegroom's boot. And then, after lunch, Mike took to the field again – for a different team. A case, as one touchline wag put it, of leaving the bride with sweet FA.

King James I's favourite, Philip Herbert, and his bride were another couple who were allowed no peace on the morning after their wedding. But they were at least able to stay in bed. The monarch suddenly appeared in their room and leapt into the four-poster with them for a right royal romp.

Two other kings were apparently able to enter neither into the honeymoon spirit nor their brides. In the eleventh century, Editha, wife of Edward the Confessor,

. . . and leapt into the four-poster with them for a right royal romp.

refused to consummate her marriage on the bizarre grounds that this would be an ideal way to test her husband's ability to withstand temptation.

Perhaps Editha was inspired by the example of Audrey, who wed King Egfrid of Northumbria in the seventh century. She is said to have remained a virgin all her life, although she married twice. Audrey finally became Abbess of Ely and took a bath three times a year - strictly to mortify her flesh.

An Essex bridegroom, Andrew Woodhead, found himself in a ridiculous - and painful - position on his wedding night.

His bride Carol had gone up to bed feeling woozy after the reception and fallen into a deep sleep. Meanwhile Andrew gallantly nipped out to find a taxi for some of the guests.

But when he had said goodbye to his friends, he found himself locked out of the house. He decided to climb in through the bedroom window and perhaps give his bride a little romantic surprise. Halfway up, he bashed his nose on a central heating vent and plummeted to the ground.

Said Carol later:

'Unbeknown to us, our neighbour was killing herself with laughter watching the whole thing. It was terribly embarrassing when we held a barbecue the following evening, and she told everyone how we'd spent our wedding night.'

The 7th Earl of Aberdeen and his wife Ishbel embarked upon a most elaborate honeymoon after their wedding in 1877. The trip lasted more than six months and included a cruise down the Nile and visits to Paris and the Italian

Alps. But disaster can strike even the most gilded of couples, and the Aberdeens' grand tour was blighted almost before it got underway.

Two days after their wedding, the Earl and Countess were taking tea in a country house at Halstead, Kent, which they had been lent for the first few days of their life together. Suddenly the door burst open and in rushed her ladyship's German maid, all in a tizzy, and gasping the immortal words: 'Ach, gnädige Frau – Ach! Ach!'

Quite unflustered, the Earl addressed the distraught domestic.

'What is the matter; have the pipes burst?' (His lordship was well-known for his little jokes. Indeed, he told them on public platforms and embalmed many of his better cracks in books.)

But this was no time for laughter. It turned out that the Countess's dressing-room had been ransacked and her fabulous jewels had disappeared.

The Keystone Cops would have been proud of what followed. His lordship decided the thieves might still be nearby. But the nearest door leading into the garden was locked; so, in the words of the Countess: 'A. seized the poker in my room and set himself to burst the locked door open, my maid now hanging on to his coat tails and entreating him to desist or he might be murdered, and his valet standing behind him shaking like an aspen leaf.'

Pausing only to give instructions to call the local constabulary and to dictate an offer for a house in Grosvenor Square to a passing telegraph boy, Aberdeen was off in hot pursuit. But it was all in vain. The thieves, the police later established, had resorted to a wily stratagem, calculated to outwit anyone with a true sense of how things were done. They escaped by train, but a trail of empty jewel-cases showed that they had caught it, as the Countess rather sniffily noted, at St Mary Cray, 'a station on the Chatham line, whereas the regular station for Halstead was on the South Eastern'.

Almost a century later, in May 1981, the Aberdeens' great grandson Alexander Gordon, now Earl of Haddo, took his wife Joanna to Elba for their honeymoon.

The island proved to be an ideal choice – sunshine, beautiful beaches, and excellent restaurants in which to sample the local cuisine.

Only one thing seemed a little odd: the islanders appeared keen to get everything done early. In the afternoon, they would leave the beach a good hour before Alexander and Joanna felt necessary, and at night the restaurants were empty well before the Gordons had finished their dinner.

They put it all down to some quaint local custom.

As it happened, some relations of Joanna's sister-in-law were in the same village, and generously invited the honeymooners to lunch in a local restaurant. They arranged to meet at one o'clock.

Good manners demanded that Alexander and Joanna should not be late, and they made sure that they reached the restaurant on time. Their hosts were already there, and Alexander noticed that they seemed strangely relieved to see them, as though, for some reason, they had been afraid their guests would not turn up. But nothing was said, and an excellent lunch was quickly served.

A few days later, another odd thing happened. The honeymooners decided to visit one of Elba's tourist attractions, Napoleon's house. Alexander consulted the guidebook which said that the house closed at three. So at two, they presented themselves at the entrance, looking forward to an hour's sight-seeing.

To their surprise and irritation, the custodian would not let them in. The house, he said, was closed.

Alexander began to argue. Wasn't the house not due to shut till three?

The custodian stood his ground.

Alexander showed him the closing time in the guide-book.

The custodian remained unmoved.

Alexander showed him his watch.

This finally brought a reaction from the custodian.

He showed Alexander his watch.

Alexander's watch showed that it was just past two.

The custodian's watch made it just past three.

So someone was an hour out. But who?

It was then that the truth dawned. Could this explain why the restaurants seemed to close early, why the other people on the beach seemed to go home when there was still an hour's bathing-time left, why there had been a slight 'atmosphere' when they had arrived for lunch with their friends?

It could. It did. But how had they managed to be one hour out of step with the rest of Elba?

Alexander thought back, and remembered.

Now although he's a very up-to-date sort of fellow, his watch is slightly old-fashioned. It's not powered by a battery, but is wound and rewound by the movement of its wearer's wrist. This means that if it is not worn for some time, it will stop.

And this is what had happened on the first day of the honeymoon, after Alexander had taken it off on the beach. When he had reset it, he had taken the time from Joanna's watch.

Now Joanna has one of those watches with no figures to mar its elegance. So it can be difficult for someone else to tell exactly where the hour hand is pointing. Alexander had got it wrong. He had set his watch one hour behind. It was, you might say, a timely reminder of what a honeymoon is for: a chance to get used to your spouse - and her watch.

Mrs Susan Sweet of Middlesex owns what must be one of the strangest-ever honeymoon souvenirs.

She acquired it when she went shopping six days after her marriage. While she was parking her car, another woman drove up and claimed the parking place was hers.

Mrs Sweet was then hit in the face as she sat in her Metro. The blow broke her nose.

After her assailant had been fined by a court, Mrs Sweet said:

'My nose was so painful that my husband and I couldn't kiss for the whole of our honeymoon.'

And she also described that strange souvenir:

'I kept the plaster cast which I had on my nose as a souvenir of our honeymoon, and we keep it as a memento on our dressing-table.'

Trust the South Americans to introduce the strangest elements into honeymoons.

Brazilian bride Maria Duarte got into a prize political pickle after winning a sweeping victory in her local council elections. She polled three thousand votes more than her nearest rival.

Imagine the sensation, therefore, when Maria's mother announced to her daughter's supporters at the victory dinner that Miss Duarte would not, after all, be taking up her seat.

For in between the campaign and the count, Maria had got married – to a rival candidate, Mr Adolph Filho, who had polled only 425 votes. Now Mr Filho was refusing to allow his bride to leave the matrimonial home for any reason.

During the campaign Maria and Adolph had publicly disagreed upon a fundamental question. Surprisingly, her party believed that a woman's place was in the home, while Adolph's preached liberation and argued that women should be allowed to have their own careers.

And that is why, such are the strange ways of South American politics, everyone was happy with this announcement issued by Maria from her honeymoon hotel:

> I chose love. I would give Adolph my seat if that was possible. He has explained everything to me. I see that women must be allowed to play their part in moulding the aspirations of the community to which they belong.

An odd thing also happened to Mr Andrew Prosser who spent his honeymoon on the Isle of Wight a year or two ago. While browsing in an antique shop, he noticed an attractive old plate with a picture of a local castle painted on it and bought it for £15. Andrew had intended to give it to his bride, but changed his mind and presented it instead to his mother.

By all accounts, Mother was more touched by the thought than by the beauty of the plate, but she hung it on the wall all the same.

Then, one day, she realised the plate was exceptionally

well painted, and when she went to up to London she popped into the auction rooms at Christie's to have it appraised.

The experts were ecstatic, for the honeymoon souvenir was no less than a trial plate made by Wedgwood in the 1770s after Catherine the Great of Russia (to console herself no doubt after her own honeymoon disaster) had ordered a special dinner service. It fetched a cool £8,640 at auction.

Many of the oddest honeymoon disasters have that most mundane of causes – a row between the newlyweds. Here are a couple of examples from my file of the furious.

Everything started off well for Istvan Havas of Miskolc in Hungary. After the wedding ceremony he carried his radiant bride Marcia over the threshold of their new flat. The trouble began when Istvan announced that he didn't like her choice of green curtains.

The bride was furious. A tempestuous row ensued. Finally, Istvan stormed out of their new home.

But when he reached the street below, he was stopped by his wife who, in conciliatory mood, leaped out of the second-floor window. Her aim was excellent, but she broke her neck and Istvan's leg when she landed on him.

But all's well that ends well, and the quarrelling couple were reunited in adjoining hospital beds.

Marvar Stephen had planned a dream trip to the Caribbean. The tickets were booked, the cases packed, but just after the wedding, Marvar and her new husband began to argue. It turned into a real humdinger of a row, and finally the bride flew off alone to the West Indies.

Her aim was excellent . . .

When Marvar got home, she was met at the airport by her husband . . . and his new girlfriend.

Finally, one of the oddest honeymoon memories of all. Mrs R. Green of Dundee shared the joke with readers of a Sunday newspaper. She wrote:

> The only thing my dear husband ever remembers about our honeymoon is . . . 'a lovely blonde was at our hotel'. Not me, folks, I'm a brunette.

To practical jokers, honeymooners present an easy target, and there is no one more easily fooled than a bridegroom who has had too wild a stag night.

For example, doctors like to tell of one of their number who passed out in a drunken stupor on the eve of his wedding and awoke to find his leg in plaster up to the thigh. He naturally believed his friends – they *were* doctors, after all – when they said he'd met with an accident while he was tired and emotional.

The problem was that it was winter-time and the newlyweds had booked a skiing holiday. So the melancholy medic had to spend his fortnight's honeymoon standing shivering on a Swiss mountainside watching his wife speed over the snow.

It was not until the bridegroom got back home to

Britain and went to the orthopaedic clinic that he realized he had fallen for one of the oldest medical pranks in the book. He had not broken his leg at all. It was simply a case of getting plastered while plastered.

Gerald Tyrwhitt-Wilson, Lord Berners, is said to have perpetrated a fiendishly elaborate hoax upon an unsuspecting honeymoon couple who had borrowed his house overlooking the Forum in Rome.

Berners, who enjoyed a practical joke, carefully collected the visiting cards of all the most crashing bores in London.

He then let his butler in on the secret and instructed him to present the cards to the couple at varying intervals during their stay.

The honeymooners were aghast as card after card was borne to them on the statutory silver tray, and spent most of their stay frantically dodging the 'visitors' instead of partaking of the delights of the Eternal City.

And spare a thought (for a change) for the dreaded Cesare Borgia. It is said that at his wedding someone managed to slip some powerful laxatives into his celebration drink, with the inevitable result that Cesare had to spend most of the night in the loo rather than in rapture.

Cesare was less than amused, but then whoever expected a Borgia to see the funny side of things?

You'll have realised by now that there is a golden rule which every bride and groom must accept: when you get hitched you get hitches.

For some unfortunate couples disasters come in droves.

For instance, Yorkshirewoman Helen Hird suffered a triple calamity when she went on her honeymoon in supposedly innocuous Cornwall.

'I lost my voice on my wedding night through tonsilitis,' she said, 'so I took some penicillin on honeymoon and immediately developed an eye infection.

'Then, to cap it all, I fell down three times on the same day, landing heavily on my arm while walking on the cliff top.'

Sensibly, the hoodooed Helen returned home four days early – to avoid further disasters.

So many things went wrong for Karen and Steve Price in the run-up to their wedding that they didn't dare contemplate a honeymoon in case that, too, turned out to be jinxed. Here is their catalogue of calamity:

The firm from which Karen had ordered her wedding dress went bust, and she had to scrabble about in a bailiff's dust-choked warehouse to retrieve it.

The hall where they had planned to hold the reception turned out to have been double-booked.

They had hired a Rolls Royce as a bridal car, but it was vandalised.

When the bridesmaids' dresses arrived they were the wrong size and had to be remade.

The caterer fell ill and could not prepare the wedding feast, and the disco the couple had lined up for a dance with 200 guests went out of business.

'I just couldn't believe our bad luck,' said Karen after the marriage ceremony. 'At least the service went off without a hitch.'

'But we're not taking any chances with a honeymoon abroad.'

Paul and Sandra Greenfield of Reading did risk a honeymoon, but it must have been overshadowed by the extraordinary chapter of accidents that preceded it.

It all began on the eve of the wedding when Paul left a pile of presents on his car roof. And of course he forgot all about them and drove off. They were never seen again. Next he lost a diamond from his engagement ring.

To everyone's relief, the wedding service went smoothly, but fire broke out at the reception because of an electrical fault. Seventy guests took to their heels.

Although the firemen rescued the wedding cake, the rest of the food was lost and had to be replaced by a chicken take-away. Then Sandra's parents were in a car crash as they drove from the reception.

Finally, when Paul and Sandra stopped off at their home they found water from a burst pipe cascading through the front door.

A stark choice faced them: to stay at home and stem the flood or to risk the honeymoon they had planned. They choose the latter and wisely left their relatives to mop up.

. . . Paul left a pile of presents on his car roof.

When film star Henry Fonda married Margaret Sullavan in Baltimore in 1931, there was barely time to cut the wedding cake before the bridegroom was due on stage for an afternoon matinée of *The Ghost Train*.

Only later, when the play had ended its run, were the Fondas able to go away together. Though he had little money, Fonda decided to do it in style. He bought a car, a Stutz Bearcat, and in it one morning they chugged towards Virginia. But thirty miles out, the ricketty car broke down and would not budge. It had reached journey's end - and so, too, had the Fondas. All their money had gone on the clapped-out Bearcat, and they had trouble scraping together enough cash for two bus tickets. And these only took them a short distance - back to where they had come from, a hotel in Baltimore. The only consolation was that they arrived in time for lunch.

In a newspaper column, Alan Williams told readers of the *Mail on Sunday* in December 1985 about a near-fatal honeymoon journey nearly twenty years earlier. He and his bride were hoping to fly between Bangkok and Phnom-Penh, the capital of Cambodia.

'The plane', he wrote, 'belonged to Cambodia's new national airline - now defunct - whose maiden flight had vanished a few months earlier somewhere over the jungle, with the loss of all twenty VIPs on board.

'The flight I boarded with my new bride was very nearly our last, when the pilot - who, it turned out later, was under the influence of whisky and opium at the time - raised the undercarriage before take-off.

'We only survived because of the Dakota's almost indestructible framework.'

John and Mary Beresford picked the romantic Highlands of Scotland for what turned out to be a bad news/good news honeymoon. It was a long drive from their home in Lancashire, but all went well until they reached Inverness, eight hours into the journey. Suddenly, on a lonely road, a tyre burst. There was much more bad news to come. The couple changed the wheel, only to find that the spare was punctured too.

John rang the R.A.C. who explained that it would take some time to provide spares since it was a Sunday afternoon and Highland garagemen take the Sabbath very seriously. Five hours later, however, the couple were back on their way again, with their honeymoon village in Sutherland only 130 miles away.

Worse was to happen the following day. The Beresfords took a trip to Thurso, but on the way they collided with another car, badly denting their offside wing.

Then Mary bought a bottle of best malt whisky to cheer her husband up, but, as she presented it to him, it slipped from his hands and shattered on the pavement.

Mary said, 'Never mind, our luck is bound to change,' but no one believed her.

That was all the bad news.

For the good news they had to wait until three days before the end of the honeymoon. It came when they bought an instant lottery ticket, and Mary's optimism was justified. Mary and John had won the top prize of £1,000, and the distinction of providing one of the very few pieces of good news in this book.

As every schoolkid knows, there was no more belligerent or successful basher of the Romans than Attila the Hun. Not for nothing was he known as the 'Scourge of God' as he scythed his way across Europe with his hordes.

Attila seemed unstoppable. City after city and country after country fell to him. And, like every great soldier, he managed to die in bed. The only problem was that his timing was none too good, for the infamous Hun met his end on his wedding night in A D 453.

Legend has it that the amorous Attila (he had several wives) was so overexcited by his new bride that he died of a burst artery. It is also said that Mrs Attila, in her turn, was so horrified by her husband's unexpected demise that she did not dare call for help for a full twenty-four hours.

Not a bad way to go, you might say, but Attila's honeymoon haemorrhage was not merely a disaster for him. After his funeral, the Hunnish undertakers who made the burial arrangements were all executed so that Attila might enjoy in death something that he had failed to give the rest of Europe in his lifetime - peace.

Death on honeymoon is, of course, the ultimate disaster, as Miss Margaret Lofty would have testified - if she had survived to tell the tale.

... the infamous 'Brides in the Bath' murderer.

In 1914 the trusting Miss Lofty married a man who called himself 'John Lloyd'. He had a curious habit of asking the landladies of rooms he wished to rent about the washing facilities.

Now 'John Lloyd', quite unknown to Miss Lofty of course, was none other than George Joseph Smith the infamous 'Brides in the Bath' murderer. 'Mrs Lloyd's' honeymoon, therefore, was clean, warm, wet ... and very short.

Peter Bowler and Jonathon Green, in their ghoulishly hilarious catalogue of bizarre deaths *What A Way To Go!*, tell an extraordinary story of a bride who met an untimely end in the early years of the nineteenth century.

After dinner at a wedding party in Norfolk, the guests began a game of hide and seek. The bride joined in enthusiastically, and, despite being encumbered with her wedding finery, she took her turn to hide.

But no one could find her. At first her friends and family admired the skill with which she had managed to conceal herself. Then, when she still had not turned up, they became a little more worried and scoured the house for her.

Still the bride could not be found. Finally, after many hours had passed, panic set in. The wedding party, under the direction of a by now frantic bridegroom, turned the place inside out - or so they thought. In the end, they had to give up.

Somehow - and neither Messrs Bowler and Green nor history relate how - the bridegroom quickly became reconciled to the mysterious disappearance of his beloved, and, after a suitable period of mourning, returned to Real Life.

Three years later, back in the house where the wedding party had been held, someone chanced to prise open the lid of an old chest. A ghastly sight met their eyes, for there lay the skeleton of a woman clad in a mouldering wedding dress.

It turned out that the bride had indeed hidden herself well. What she had not realised was that the chest had a spring lock which, once closed, could not be opened from inside. And the wood of the chest had been too thick for her cries for help to be heard.

And then there was a Mr Oliver Leonard, who was unwise enough to marry a widow called Mrs Wilson. Leonard keeled over and expired suspiciously soon after the wedding.

It was then that people began to talk. Hadn't the widow Wilson's first husband died very soon after her first marriage ceremony? And hadn't the new Mrs Leonard replied, when someone asked what to do with the eats left over from the reception: 'Just keep them for the funeral, although I might give this one a week's extension'?

Further investigation revealed that poor Mr Leonard had been poisoned with phosphorus, and the homicidal honeymooner duly met her come-uppance.

In Colorado Springs, Colorado, in 1982, a bridegroom was killed before the honeymoon could begin. He died at the hands of his mother-in-law, but not as a result of the enmity that all too often arises between a mother and the Man Not Worthy Enough To Tie The Shoelaces of her beautiful daughter.

Apparently there was a row at the reception. Mom reached for her shotgun which she had somehow concealed about her person.

Then Mom let fly with both barrels, and the bridegroom died simply because he got in the way. Mom had really meant to hit her own husband.

Finally, in 1923, George Ives, an Edwardian eccentric who collected bizarre newspaper cuttings, clipped this poignant tale of the honeymoon couple who brought disaster upon themselves. And for a really unusual reason: they were actually enjoying their first few days of wedded bliss. Far too much, sad to say.

Six days after their wedding, Monsieur Paul Albert Liebaut and his bride Germaine were found dead at their home in Suresnes near Paris.

The police deduced that Germaine, who was attired for the occasion in her wedding dress, had first shot her husband before turning the gun upon herself.

The bride had obviously been a considerate girl, for she had left a strange note for the police who published these extracts:

> We are killing ourselves because we are too happy.
>
> We do not need money, for we are worth over 30,000 francs.
>
> We have good health and a wonderful future before us, but we prefer to die now because we are the happiest people in the world.
>
> We adore each other, but we would rather descend into the grave together while we are still so happy.

If that's what happiness did to them, think what might have happened if the Liebauts, like the other people in this book, had suffered a honeymoon disaster. On the other hand, it might have saved their lives . . .

A strange and tragic story caught my eye the other day as I was reading *The Times*. It concerned a double wedding party in Turkey - two brothers had married two sisters. Both brides and grooms and many of their guests came to grief on the journey between the wedding ceremony and the reception.

Usually, people have no more than a short distance to travel from the church or registry office, but these Turks had to travel a staggering *350 miles* to the party. On the way, their bus collided with a lorry in fog.

Now that doesn't give us anything to laugh about, but to journey so far after a wedding is really taking a chance. Perhaps the tragic Turks - who after all had thought twice already and married sisters - would have thought twice again if they'd only known how often accidents befall even the most prudent of honeymooners.

The Times used to take a great interest in accidents sustained before the honeymoon began, and which inevitably cast a blight on the days ahead.

In 1958, with true British understatement, the paper's New York correspondent reported that 'a wedding on Saturday at Rochester, New York, is to have some unusual features'. In fact, the man from the Big Apple had hit upon the first known story of a 'broken' marriage occurring before the actual ceremony.

The report went on to explain:

> The bride, Miss Suzanne Archibald, will be wearing a splint on her foot because of a toe broken in a motoring accident; the bridegroom, Mr Edward Stanton, knocked unconscious in the same accident, is still suffering from concussion, and the maid of honour, who was also in the accident, has a black eye and a sprained ankle. Two of the bridesmaids, victims of skating accidents, have each an arm in a sling, one because of a fractured humerus, the other because of a dislocated shoulder.

Many years earlier, the 'Thunderer' had carried a cautionary tale from the church of St James the Less in Bethnal Green, London.

The kindly vicar there had been in the habit of conducting weddings free of charge, and, to add to the happy atmosphere, guests used to line up outside the building and throw rice at the bride and groom. For the grocers of Bethnal Green it was a bonanza, but all too often the couple on the receiving end of the rice shower came in for a painful peppering.

We'll let *The Times* reporter continue the story:

> The brides are generally protected by their veils, the bridegrooms are less fortunate, and yesterday one of them received several grains in his eyes. When he raised his arm to shield himelf a fresh fusillade was opened upon him, and it was only when he staggered back in pain that it dawned upon his friends that they

The bride . . . will be wearing a splint on her foot . . .

had given him a reception with more vigour than discretion. After a vain attempt to clear his eyes he was led to a surgery adjacent, and he will now have to pass in the ward of a hospital what would have been his honeymoon.

Bridget Gorman of Portsmouth, Hampshire, also had to visit hospital on her wedding day – thanks to the fact that her wedding ring was left in a drawer at home in a pre-service mix-up.

There was no time to go home and fetch it, but bridegroom Robert Singleton managed to borrow his sister's ring and the ceremony was able to go ahead. In time-honoured tradition, the ring was lovingly placed upon the third finger of the bride's left hand. And there it stuck – fast. Not only could Bridget not remove it, but the bothersome band was far too tight.

She was driven straight from the service to hospital, her finger by now badly swollen.

The appearance at the casualty ward of a bride in full gown and veil caused a sensation, and of course inspired even more tender loving treatment than usual as the ring was sawn off.

Said Bridget later on: 'I was so embarrassed, but the nurses were very good. I didn't have to queue at casualty.'

But despite the doctors' speedy sawing, Bridget still missed the reception. And she even temporarily missed out on her honeymoon, for later Robert's car broke down and the cut-up couple had to postpone the trip.

American Robert Graf Jr from Connecticut had a real lump in his throat during his marriage to Karen Nebor, but not for the usual emotional reasons. For earlier, during breakfast, a piece of sausage had stuck in Robert's throat. Try as he could, he was quite unable to dislodge it.

At the local medical centre the doctors wrestled with the blocking banger, but it was jammed fast.

The day wore on, and the hour fixed for the wedding drew near. Gallantly, although he was in pain, Robert decided that he could not let Karen down and staggered to the altar of Killingworth Congregational Church, where the Reverend William Gaydos ensured that the knot was tied in record time.

Then, instead of setting off on honeymoon or even enjoying the reception, the bridegroom was rushed to a nearby hospital where the offending sausage was finally removed.

Describing the wedding later, the bride's sister, Geri Nebor, said: 'It was a beautiful ceremony. Everyone was crying.'

Every bride dreads being buttonholed by a guest. Yet that is what happened – with a vengeance – to Susan Merricks of Martinsvale, Virginia in August 1982. It meant that she, too, had to substitute a visit to hospital for a honeymoon.

Disaster struck when the affectionate Susan embraced one of the wedding party. If only she had noticed that the guest was wearing a buttonhole, fixed with a sharp pin ... As it turned out, such was the enthusiasm of Susan's hug that the pin penetrated her chest and punctured one of her lungs.

A Greek bride's honeymoon was spoiled when pins which a seamstress had carelessly left in her wedding gown penetrated her bottom. She was so sore that she was unable to sit down at her wedding reception.

The sloppy seamstress was quickly brought to justice. She pleaded pressure of business, but the court decided that no bride should have to do duty as a pin cushion and imposed a fine.

John and Maxine Hurley of London achieved the ambition of most honeymoon couples: they spent almost all their time in bed. But they had to, for they caught food poisoning at their wedding reception.

The reception had been a slap-up do with five hundred guests tucking in to a feast at a restaurant. It was only when John and Maxine reached romantic Venice, their base for a three-week honeymoon, that they realised something was wrong.

'Our holiday was a nightmare,' said Maxine. 'We spent most of it in bed being ill and rushing to the toilet.'

Meanwhile back in England, two hundred of the guests were also suffering. Maxine revealed: 'So many guests were taken ill, hospitals were turning people away.'

And even when the queasy couple finally got home their troubles were not over, for Maxine's hair started to fall out.

Happily, by the time the case came to court, Maxine and John proved they had also had time to succumb to something else – the love bug – and had produced a baby daughter.

It wasn't the food that upset Madge Riley at her reception, but the champagne – or rather one of the bottles it came in.

She and her husband Tony had been given a special presentation pack of bubbly and two glasses, and they had decided to save it up for breakfast after their wedding night.

But suddenly, just as Madge was saying goodbye to one of the last of the wedding guests, the pack fell off the table and the bottle exploded, showering the bride with bubbles and broken glass.

'I don't remember much about it,' she said, 'except feeling something in my foot.'

She was rushed to hospital where her left leg was encased in plaster. The doctors insisted she should stay there overnight.

Husband Tony, meanwhile, had to sleep in a separate guest room – enough to take the fizz out of anyone's wedding night.

Mused Madge philosophically: 'Tony did promise to love, honour and obey in sickness and in health, but I don't think he expected it to be this soon.'

Kenneth and Donna Kiehn gave a whole new meaning to the phrase 'falling in love' when they agreed to pose for 'just one more' photograph at their reception.

There they were looking all lovey-dovey and saying 'cheese' when they fell off the balcony on which they were sitting and crashed thirty feet into a decorative fountain below.

'They will have a long recovery period,' the bride's mother told a solicitous reporter. 'They were still holding hands when we pulled them out.'

If they survive the reception, newlyweds seem to stand a pretty good chance of making it to their wedding night unscathed. Though not always. The old, and, perhaps fortunately, dying custom of accompanying the bride and groom to the station to ensure that they catch their honeymoon train has led to more than one honeymoon coming to an end almost before it has begun.

Scottish newspaper columnist Pearl Murray regaled her readers with this story some years ago:

> Exuberant wedding guests, accompanying a couple to the station to see them off on honeymoon, lifted the poor bridegroom off his feet and tossed him in the air a few times.
>
> But the bridegroom was not exactly robust – and he set off on his honeymoon semi-conscious.

Perhaps a certain smugness on the part of some brides and grooms that they have sailed quite happily over the marriage hurdles so far leads them to become a little careless on the actual wedding night itself, for this is a time when bizarre and painful accidents all too often come about.

Peter Kinnell, in his amusing *Book of Erotic Failures*, recounts this story of a certain 'well-known Fleet Street editor's' wedding night.

Apparently, the editor (whom Kinnell sensitively does

. . . he set off on his honeymoon semi-conscious.

not name) was making love to his bride when he somehow managed to get his foot stuck in the bars of the bedroom electric fire.

The fire was on at the time, and in seconds the sizzling scribe was writhing in agony. His bride, oblivious to what had really happened, was immensely gratified: from his gyrations and groans she assumed she was giving him an ecstatic time.

And it was not until her husband broke free – both of her and the bars of the electric fire – and clutched his smouldering foot that she realised the truth.

Readers of *The News of the World* revealed these intimate disasters when the paper offered a prize for the best 'honeymoon howlers'.

Mr C. Williams of Bristol wrote to say that his wedding night was such hot stuff that he decided to get out of bed to open a window to let in the cool night air.

'But as I did – crash! The sash cords snapped and I was trapped by my fingers. I wasn't hurt, just unable to get free.'

Mr Williams and his bride tried everything, but after an hour there was nothing for it: the bride had to call the police. They proved to be perfect gentlemen and immensely discreet.

'She opened the front door of the boarding house and two cops and two firemen tiptoed in.

'To spare our blushes they didn't wake anyone as they prised me free with iron bars. But it was no joke on our honeymoon,' said Mr Williams.

Mrs B. Keen wrote this one-sentence letter from Sussex.

It certainly gives the impression that there was no more to be said about her wedding night:

> A romantic dinner on our wedding night dished my husband's passion – he spilt a hot bowl of soup in his lap.

And Mrs Ann Polhill from Nottinghamshire had a similar tale to tell of pain, passion, and a little pride:

> A wasp flew up my husband's trouser leg on our honeymoon and stung him in a delicate spot. For the rest of our stay he had a bad limp. Guests eyed us with awe.

Even when the wedding night is over, it can be most unwise for a honeymooning couple to become complacent about avoiding accidents, as Nigel Crowther-Jones can affirm.

Nigel, from Wiltshire, was lucky enough to honeymoon on the beautiful island of St Lucia in the West Indies. His bad luck was to be cut by the tail of a stingray as he swam in the warm and otherwise welcoming waters of the Caribbean Sea.

An even more embarrassing fate overtook Richard Hopkins of Peterborough. He, too, honeymooned in an exotic spot – Barbados – though it did him little good. Like Nigel Crowther-Jones, Richard met disaster while swimming. A speedboat ran over him and gashed his bottom so badly that he needed 19 stitches. As a result, the rueful Richard had to spend the rest of the trip lying on his front being consoled by his wife Sally.

A good friend of mine who got married in the tropics came to grief because, following the example of mad dogs and other Englishmen, he went out in the midday sun.

After the wedding, the party went on long into the night. When it finally finished, my friend, who had generously laid on an ocean of booze, was capable only of crawling into bed to sleep it all off.

When he awoke next morning, the tropical sun was already high in the sky. His lovely bride was already awake, taking the air in the garden.

As he watched her, a dreadful realisation crept over my friend. The marriage had not been consummated!

So my friend and his bride met in the garden.

He said to her: 'What about it?'

She said to him: 'Let's not wait a second longer.'

And the consequence was that my friend couldn't sit down for days afterwards, thanks to a badly sunburnt bottom . . .

David Bryant was unfortunate enough to have his honeymoon accident recorded on video for posterity. His bride Philippa was photographing him as he posed at the edge of a cliff. Suddenly, David toppled over the edge and fell 50 feet into the Avon Gorge.

Innocently, Philippa kept the camera rolling and even

zoomed in on her husband's by now contorted face. It was only when she found focus that she realised something was wrong.

'I thought he was laughing,' she said later. 'In fact he was screaming with pain.'

Poor old David was not badly hurt, but he had sustained that most inconvenient of honeymoon injuries, a pain in the groin.

By this time, Philippa was distraught, and on hearing that David was being kept in hospital, she fainted. When she recovered, she was more philosophical:

'The damage should be better soon,' she said, 'but at the moment David's in a rather delicate state – which is unfortunate on our honeymoon. But at least he's all right. I suppose you could say he fell for me in a big way!'

Here's another story which features a fall. The difference is that *both* newlyweds went flying.

Geoff and Barbara Clinton-Jones from Middlesbrough booked a luxury honeymoon in Rome, and very little went right for them from the moment they stepped off the plane.

First there was a mix-up over the hire-car they had ordered. That took them a day on the telephone, much arm-waving and £25-worth of taxis to sort out.

And when they did finally set off, a tyre sprang a puncture just a few miles along the road. As Geoff wrestled with the spare tyre, a hooded motorcyclist sped up and snatched Barbara's handbag. In it were her jewellery and spending money.

Reporting the honeymoon highwayman to the local constabulary took four hours and visits to two police stations.

By now the couple were worn out and their spirits low.

. . . a hooded motorcyclist sped up and snatched Barbara's handbag.

What could be more cheering, they thought, than dinner at a romantic little restaurant?

A suitable hostelry was near at hand, and they gratefully took their seats at a table on the verandah. The evening was like velvet, and Geoff and Barbara were contentedly soaking up the *ambiance* – when the verandah collapsed. Barbara plunged halfway through the floor and had to be pulled free.

The couple managed to avoid further accidents until they got back to the airport after a tour of the country. Stashed in the boot of their car was £800-worth of souvenirs and gifts – all of which was stolen while they had a cup of coffee.

Then their flight back to Britain was held up by a radar fault, and when they finally made it through the front door of their home, they found that a bathroom tank had burst and water was dripping through the ceiling.

Said Barbara with understandable emotion: 'I could have wept. It was a memorable honeymoon ... for all the wrong reasons.'

Karen Wright and her husband Nicolas from Yorkshire also met with double disaster.

A few days after their marriage at St Anne's Cathedral in Leeds, the Wrights flew to Spain for what promised to be an exotic eleven-day honeymoon.

They reached their hotel just outside Torremolinos in the evening, and, after unpacking, decided to go out for a meal.

They found they had to cross a dual carriageway to get to the restaurant. What they did not know was that to do so was highly dangerous and that there was a subway for pedestrians.

Their other mistake was to forget to look in the right direction while they were crossing. In Yorkshire cars drive on the left, but not in Spain . . .

Halfway across, Karen and Nicolas were hit by a car. Nicolas was flung onto its bonnet, shattering the windscreen, but amazingly suffered only cuts and bruises.

Karen came off much worse. She was rushed to hospital where doctors diagnosed a fractured skull.

Nicolas was allowed out next day, but Karen had to stay on in her sickbed. When she eventually left hospital, there were only five days of her honeymoon left, and she was in too much pain to enjoy them.

Back in Leeds, Karen asked the doctors why her right leg was so sore. They pondered their diagnosis. Had she sustained a sprain in Spain? Well no she hadn't: her leg in fact was broken.

Fortunately, Karen has now fully recovered and says: 'I laugh at it all now, but it wasn't so funny at the time.'

And when I asked her what she felt about her disastrous honeymoon, she put into words what so many people in this book must have felt:

'I feel as though I've been cheated out of one. I'd like to have another honeymoon – but you never can.'

The 'literature' of honeymoons – i.e. the books and newspaper cuttings consulted by people like me – is full of the strangest quotes. Consider this one, for example. It comes from a learned tome called *The Sexual Life of*

Woman by E. Heinrich Kisch MD. Dr Kisch asserts:

'According to the observations of Schule, young married hysterical women not infrequently run away with a waiter during the honeymoon journey.'

It certainly makes you think. How did this chap Schule find out such a remarkable fact? Did he spend a lot of time conducting interviews in restaurants and hotel dining-rooms? What do waiters have to offer that an ordinary husband doesn't? And what prompts the women to take flight – not just simple hysteria surely?

Actually, I can think of one thing that might make any bride bolt: an unromantic honeymoon. The whole idea of the thing, after all, is that it should be an idyllic interlude before the realities of life crowd in. Yet many couples, either by accident or design, spend the first few hours and days of their marriage in the most unromantic of circumstances. Fortunately, the newlyweds in the stories that follow have stoically accepted their lot – some even claim to have enjoyed it. And not one of the brides appears to have eloped with a waiter.

Unromantic honeymoons are nothing new. In the seventeenth century, astronomer Edmond Halley spent several nights of his honeymoon away from the nuptial bed in his Islington observatory charting the progress of 'his' comet.

And there is an odd tale told of Richard Porson, a brilliant but eccentric Regius Professor of Greek at Cambridge. Porson married a Mrs Lunan in 1796. The wedding took place in the morning, and as soon as the ceremony was over, the bride and groom went their separate ways. Porson took lunch with a friend and apparently did not once mention his marriage. He went on to spend the evening with another friend, and then, as was his habit after dinner, the peculiar professor repaired to his club.

In this century, film-star Mary Pickford also spent what should have been her honeymoon pretending that nothing in her life had changed. This was because she had married her first husband, Owen Moore, in secret, and did not want her family to know.

So Mary spent her wedding night at home in the room she shared with her sister, after bidding her husband goodnight at the front door. Months later, she confessed the truth to her family, and their horrified reaction blighted a sea voyage to Cuba which was to have been the couple's long-postponed honeymoon. It turned out, Mary Pickford wrote later, to be 'more like a funeral'.

For another great star, opera singer Maria Callas, work had to take precedence over honeymoon romance. So on the day after her wedding in 1949, she left her husband at home in Italy and sailed off to sing in three productions in Argentina.

But if you think that's unromantic, consider the case of America's sweetheart, actress and singer Doris Day, who married for the first time in 1941 when she was only 17.

Shortly after the wedding ceremony in New York, the bridegroom, musician Al Jorden, had to rush off to play in a show, while the dutiful Doris spent the afternoon trying to clean the grimy apartment they had rented – with a scrubbing brush, wire wool and, sadly, little success.

Happiest of recent brides treated to what to outsiders would appear to be the most unromantic of honeymoons

. . . Maureen's honeymoon was spent on the pub outing.

was probably Maureen Hodkin of Blackburn, Lancashire. When she got married in 1983, her new husband Barry took thirty drinking pals from a local pub on the trip to Blackpool. Or rather it was the other way round: Maureen's honeymoon was spent on the pub outing.

'I didn't want to miss out on the pub trip,' said Barry. Fortunately, Maureen found the excursion an enjoyable change.

'I've been married four times,' she said later, 'and this was my best honeymoon.'

Actually, in opting for companionship on their honeymoon, Maureen and Barry were in good company in more ways than one, for in 1952 the Reagans had done likewise. As they disported themselves in Phoenix, Arizona, they were joined by the bride's parents. Said Nancy afterwards: 'Having a honeymoon with your parents may seem strange to some people, but somehow it seemed perfectly natural to us.'

Cath and Martin Johnson from Durham had to spend their honeymoon with forty-nine children. They had intended to go abroad in style, but then they realised that the honeymoon would clash with an outing to London arranged by the comprehensive school at which they taught.

Generously, Cath and Martin announced that it would be easier to change their plans than the children's schedule.

Said Martin, 'When we realised the school trip and the wedding virtually coincided, we both agreed that the school trip should take priority. Anyway, we are having a lovely time.'

A Berkshire bride, Maree Dudding, set off to America for her honeymoon with husband Nigel - and twenty-nine rugby players came too.

The reason was that Nigel was committed to leading his local club on an American tour. Maree seemed quite happy to go along with both the idea and the team. 'She's a great rugby fan,' said her sister-in-law reassuringly.

Colin Copperthwaite and his new wife Kim had no option but to allow twenty-one of their wedding guests to join them on their honeymoon in Winchester.

On his stag night, Colin was set upon by his friends who locked a chain, complete with a 30 lb concrete ball, to his leg. He was even forced to hobble to his wedding at the register office with his leg still shackled. The twenty-one jokers adamantly refused to release him until he had agreed to let them acccompany him on honeymoon.

History does not relate what Kim and Colin thought of finding themselves honeymoon hostages, but after the wedding night best man Jerry Oliver, leader of the twenty-one uninvited 'honeymooners', claimed: 'We all had a good laugh, and there were no hard feelings.'

Dawn Byrne went on honeymoon with her mother and father, her grandma and her auntie, twenty-four other relatives, and, of course, her new husband Patrick. They all went to Luton Airport in a specially hired bus before flying off to Benidorm, Spain.

The idea came from the bride's mother, Mrs Joyce Stockwell, who provided the best reason I've yet heard for a family honeymoon. 'On my honeymoon', she said, 'we were on our own and in a way it was a bit boring. I thought then it would be nice to have some friends along.'

The only possible criticism of such a sensible attitude might be that it didn't go far enough. Neil and Corinne Bayliss of Northampton made doubly sure that they wouldn't be lonely by taking no fewer than ninety-seven relatives and friends with them when they honeymooned in Italy. And they were thoughtful enough to leave at least one friend behind to issue this splendidly British understatement to inquiring newspapermen: 'They like company and thought it would be fun.'

At least one clever holiday company seems to think there is a market for shared honeymoons. A firm which arranges cruises on the Norfolk Broads recently advertised a honeymoon boat. It sleeps four.

But for a really unromantic honeymoon with crowds of people, there's really only one place to go, and that, as you might expect, is behind the Iron Curtain.

In 1983 a news report on Moscow Radio described a ten-day honeymoon cruise organised for a hundred Soviet newlyweds on the Black Sea. Shipboard entertainment seems to have been strictly practical. The couples took part in a rigorous timetable of 'sex lessons' and cookery contests. They were also treated to 'talks about young families' and they were invited to meet 'doctors and other specialists'. Surveying the highlights of the cruise, the Moscow Radio reporter was happy to report that 'much fun was had in a competition for the best dish made by the young housewives'.

Sometimes newlyweds find themselves obliged to opt for a less romantic honeymoon than they might ideally have chosen.

Alison and Kevin Price of Shrewsbury cancelled their trip to Spain when their pet spaniel, Jessie, gave birth to 6 puppies. Said Alison: 'They really are very sweet. When it came to deciding on a honeymoon or the puppies, it was no contest.'

David and Julie Biddle who live in the West Midlands had planned to spend their honeymoon ski-ing in Austria after their wedding in January 1986. But instead they spent the week searching for their four-year-old black and white cat called Tonic.

Tonic had disappeared the night before the wedding, and, after the reception, when she still had not returned, the kind-hearted couple cancelled the trip and began the hunt.

Said bridegroom David: 'We are really upset. We could not bear to go away in case she returned and found no one here.'

At first things looked gloomy. The Biddles offered a reward, but false alarm followed false alarm, and Tonic was nowhere to be seen.

Then, a week after the wedding, just when David and Julie should have been returning from their honeymoon, their self-sacrifice was rewarded. Tonic turned up in a garden shed a few streets away, thinner and frightened, but little the worse for her few days as a feline fugitive.

'She'd even chosen a garden shed with an old chair in it,' Julie told me.

And what had caused her to leave home in the first place?

Tonic, of course, remains inscrutable on the subject, but Julie thinks it was because she saw them packing their bags for the honeymoon.

And when I asked a relieved Julie whether she had regretted giving up her ski-ing trip, this was her game reply: 'We saw so much snow here when we were looking for Tonic, who needs any more? We'll have a summer holiday instead.'

A happy event kept another soft-hearted couple at home in 1973, when a Teesside woman, Hilda Tonge, realised that Candy, her guinea pig, was expecting twins. Fiancé Bert agreed to cancel their planned honeymoon in Blackpool so that they could attend the birth.

Tim Taylor of Bristol was simply too busy to leave his model shop. Christmas was approaching and he had to stay to cope with the rush. 'Business comes first,' he said. 'If you don't make money you can't live.'

But that didn't mean Tim's bride, Stephanie, had to do without a honeymoon. Her new husband arranged a luxurious trip to Jersey for her – and his mother went too.

Stephanie said: 'I missed him like mad, even though I get on very well with Mrs Taylor and I had a lovely time.'

One Yorkshireman did not go on his honeymoon either – but he had no choice in the matter. In October 1981 he had been due to marry his fiancée, but he spent his honeymoon in prison instead after being remanded in custody for seven days by magistrates.

It meant that he missed not only his wedding and honeymoon, but also his fiancée's twenty-first birthday party and his stag night. But although the wedding could not take place on the appointed day, the Yorkshireman was adamant that the honeymoon should go on without him. So the bride went to Boulogne with her mother.

Said the balked bride: 'It's bitterly disappointing. Obviously I wanted my husband with me in France. But he insisted I took Mum rather than waste the tickets.'

Christine Furnell of Cambridgeshire had been looking forward to a beach honeymoon in Great Yarmouth, but a strike at the cardboard factory where her future husband, Denis, worked gave her different priorities.

So straight after the wedding, Christine joined Denis on picket duty – that most unromantic of wedding lines. Said the battling bride as she stood outside the factory with her husband: 'I'm right behind him. It wasn't how I imagined my honeymoon, but he has my full support.'

David Lee of Milton Keynes and his bride Yvonne did manage to go abroad after their wedding as they had planned. They honeymooned in Perpignan in France.

The problem was that David couldn't allow himself to be totally cut off from the rest of the world, for he was the leader of the local council and had to be in constant touch with what was happening back home.

. . . straight after the wedding, Christine joined Denis on picket duty . . .

When an emergency debate was scheduled to discuss controversial plans to privatise the city's rubbish collection service, David hopped on a plane to cast his vote.

It was a good thing he did, at least from his point of view, for the motion was passed by only one vote. Then, his duty done, back to the airport he sped and returned to the lonely Yvonne.

Sue Stockley's wedding night was spent in the cab of a tractor while her husband Mike took part in a marathon ploughing match.

Naturally, Sue hadn't planned it that way at all, but the church where she and Mike wanted to get married in Dorset suddenly became unavailable and they had to postpone the ceremony for a week.

Now the new date clashed with the ploughing match, a 24-hour furrowthon in aid of charity, and Mike had agreed to take the 3 a.m. to 9 a.m. shift.

Mike didn't want to let his friends down, and, luckily, neither did Sue.

'I know how much Mike enjoys his ploughing,' she said gamely. 'I'm an accommodating sort of lady and told him not to worry about it. But I made one condition – that I should accompany him.'

And so she did. As dawn came up over Dorset, Sue was there, and at least, unlike many a bride ensconced in a downy bed, she can say that the earth really moved on her wedding night.

A clash of dates with Southampton Boat Show totally scuppered Kim Kemp's planned honeymoon on a Greek island in 1979. She married a boat-builder, who couldn't afford to miss such an important market for his wares. Husband Bob's explanation was disarmingly honest: 'I got the dates mixed up,' he confessed.

Village cricketer David Leyland knew just what to do when he found his wedding to the club's scorer coincided with a coaching groundsman's course – he took his bride Kerry with him.

David thought the working honeymoon a wonderful idea.

'The course only comes around every two years, so I couldn't very well miss it,' David explained to a reporter.

'Then I realised it was the perfect way to start our lives together.

'After all, cricket will always mean a great deal to us. Kerry is very understanding about my passion for the game. She's always known that loving me means loving cricket as well.

'The course has been a fantastic start to our honeymoon. We've learned about keeping creases in good repair, and how to aerate a wicket properly.'

Strangely, such unromantic talk does seem to bowl a maiden over (I assume Kerry's understanding nature extends to laughing at the oldest of cricketing jokes), though the bride confessed, rather charmingly:

'I've never been able to understand why grown men get so excited about knocking a small ball around the field. But thanks to David at least I can understand the game, and keeping score helps to make matches more interesting.

'I really can't stand the game – I watch it because of love.'

Another sports-mad bridegroom, Stan Davis, promised his bride Geraldine a really romantic honeymoon when they married in 1983. Which all goes to prove that romance, like beauty, is in the eye of the beholder, for Stan had arranged to visit a spot with a special place in his heart - Aston Villa football ground in Birmingham.

Stan had emigrated to Canada, but thought his honeymoon the ideal opportunity to show Geraldine the sacred turf. Was the Aston Villa ground really worth crossing the Atlantic to see? Stan certainly thought so: 'It seems a bit odd, but I think Brum is a romantic city and we could have done worse,' he said afterwards.

Bob and Sharon Hudson of Derby changed their honeymoon booking from Wales to Blackpool in 1980. Now Blackpool is a perfectly romantic place to go to, but Bob's reason for making the change was far from dewy-eyed. He chose the North Country resort because it was the venue for a hod-carrying contest.

Fortunately, the sponsors didn't allow Bob to drop a brick where his bride was concerned, and after he'd done his 'building and cooing' in Blackpool they paid for a slap-up traditional honeymoon.

Gail Dunn's honeymoon also had a rewarding ending. Her husband Fred was mad on fishing, but she wouldn't let him go near a river at the start of their married life. Instead, Fred had to stay at their home in Blackwell Road, Carlisle.

But after three days, Gail lifted the 'No Fishing' order and Fred showed his gratitude by hooking a whopping 17 lb salmon. He sold it for £68 which, he announced, he'd put towards a more exotic honeymoon.

. . . a special place in his heart – Aston Villa football ground . . .

Said Gail: 'I didn't think fishing should be allowed on such an occasion, but after three days I said Fred could go and I'm glad I did. Now I'm looking forward to a honeymoon in the sun.'

A competitor at the annual Brass Band Championships held at the Albert Hall told a BBC Radio reporter this poignant tale in 1985.

A friend, who was an obsessively keen bandsman, got married one day. The ceremony was in the morning, and afterwards he took the bride home. Then he had his lunch, put on his uniform and went out to play in the town with the band. He came home for the tea which his new wife had prepared for him. But straight afterwards, the bandsman togged himself up in his dinner jacket and went out again, this time to perform in the evening concert.

Many years later, the wife complained to the radio interviewee: 'Are you surprised that we didn't have any family?'

Finally, here's my candidate for the title of The Bridegroom Who Spent The Least Romantic Honeymoon In History – Mr Barry Estgate of Wisbech, Cambridgeshire.

When his bride Trudy failed to turn up at the church, Barry decided not to change any of his plans. He insisted the guests should enjoy the reception and gallantly went off on honeymoon alone.

But Barry's reluctant bride was far less composed now that she was the one who had been left behind.

'I want to see him,' she announced, 'to tell him I love him and still want to marry him.'

Meanwhile Barry was finding that a solo honeymoon was not too bad after all, for his father reported:

'I've had a card from him and he says he's having a good time. He's even thinking of extending his honeymoon by another week.'

Question: What do the Queen Mother, Gloria Vanderbilt and Clive Trist have in common? Answer: They were all ill on honeymoon.

The Queen Mum had whooping cough, while Gloria Vanderbilt contracted diphtheria which put her out of action for six weeks. My friend Clive Trist spent most of his honeymoon sitting in a washbasin in an hotel in Oban, Scotland, hoping that the warm water would soothe a painful and most unromantic attack of piles!

At least they all fell ill *after* the wedding. Leon Belcher had to endure a string of embarrassing indignities to get married at all. Two days before the ceremony, Leon came down with chickenpox, and didn't exactly feel up to scratch.

Despite this irritating indisposition, to avoid disappointing his bride Sue and their guests, Leon gallantly agreed to go through with the ceremony. But he had to endure the giggles of the congregation at a particularly apt line in one of the wedding hymns:

'Finish then thy new creation, pure and spotless let us be.'

And at the reception Leon had to wear a pair of gloves to shake hands with family and friends. No spots on bride Sue, though, for her witty quote:

'After courting for five years we were itching to get married . . . but not in the way it turned out.'

There's no doubt that marriage induces strange behaviour in some people.

Take, for example, the bizarre wedding ceremony of two Americans, Mr and Mrs Mark Songer of Peoria, Illinois. Guest of honour was Mark's father - or, rather, the corpse of Mark's father.

Indeed, it was thanks to the demise of Mr Songer Senior that Mr Songer Junior got married when he did.

Mark explained on behalf of himself and his bride: 'We both wanted my father at the wedding, so when he died we decided not to wait another day and exchanged rings and vows beside the coppertone casket in which he lay, and concluded our traditional ceremony with his burial service.'

Now there's no evidence to suppose that the honeymoon that followed this oddest of weddings was disastrous in any way, but some honeymoons have been blighted by the extraordinary - occasionally even irrational - behaviour of the bride or groom.

Guest of honour was Mark's father ...

Artist Sir Stanley Spencer's nuptials at Maidenhead Registry Office in 1937 set new standards in eccentricity.

While the bride, Patricia Preece, had decked herself out in a dress and hat, Spencer turned up in a crumpled suit which had originally been made for a schoolboy. His chin was stubbly, his hair, beneath a drooping bell-shaped felt hat, unkempt, and as a finishing-touch he had donned a pair of spectacles which looked like welder's goggles.

After the ceremony, pursued by pressmen, the couple rode home on the corporation bus. When they got there, Spencer, with a cheerful 'See you later, my dear!' promptly kissed his new wife goodbye and sent her straight back to the cottage she had shared with a friend before the wedding.

The press pounced upon the tearful bride.

'Having at last decided to make ourselves respectable by marriage, we ought to have done the thing properly,' she sobbed.

Spencer clearly did not agree. He left her to spend her wedding night in the cottage, and seemed delighted next morning when he discovered that Patricia had gone on 'honeymoon' to St Ives with another woman for company.

And the reason for his happiness? He was going to spend his honeymoon with his *first* wife, who duly arrived by train that afternoon.

In November 1919 Rudolph Valentino, later to become the greatest of Hollywood heart-throbs, married actress Jean Acker. It was a whirlwind romance, and Valentino asked her to marry him. Acker accepted, although her reasons for doing so were obscure in view of the events that followed.

The newlyweds had booked into the Hollywood Hotel for their wedding night. True to age-old tradition, Valentino paused at the door of their bedroom, ready to sweep his beautiful bride into his arms, carry her over the threshold and so to bed . . .

But the beautiful bride had other ideas. She nipped into the room, slammed the door behind her and locked it. Valentino was out in the corridor and the cold.

The door stayed shut. Acker's antics proved that off-camera, at least, there was one woman who found the Great Lover of the Silver Screen highly resistible.

Another of Hollywood's most romantic stars, Jean Harlow, fared little better than the wretched Rudolph on her wedding night in 1932. Harlow was a gorgeous blonde with a ready and raunchy wit. She's the one who said: 'Every morning when I wake up I like to feel a new man.' And there were plenty of men who would have liked to oblige her.

So Harlow's announcement that she was going to marry a studio executive, Paul Bern, was greeted with disappointment and amazement. For Bern was no Hollywood hunk, but an unprepossessing fellow twice Harlow's age.

The wedding ceremony itself went off happily, but the events that followed amply fulfilled the gloomy predictions of the showbiz gossips. In the marital bedroom, Bern proved to be impotent and violent, and Harlow is said to have been covered with ugly bruises when she was finally rescued by her agent in the small hours of the morning.

Neither the marriage nor Bern recovered, and two months later the unhappy bridegroom shot himself. No

Hollywood scriptwriter could have dreamt up a better 'weepie'.

Equally odd to some people, though far less harmful, was the behaviour of King William of Orange who insisted upon keeping his woolly drawers on for his wedding night in 1677.

But I'm not so sure his attitude was wrong. It was, he explained, his habit at all times to wear his drawers to bed. His wife would simply have to get used to his foibles and it was best he should start as he meant to go on.

Sadly, history does not record whether his decision led to a honeymoon disaster or whether Mary found the royal drawers a barrier to bliss.

Sometimes a honeymoon spells disaster not for the newlyweds but for the people they encounter.

That was certainly the view taken by hoteliers in Majorca in 1980. They announced that energetic honeymooners were costing them a million pounds a year in bed repairs. One particularly athletic couple from Scotland claimed the record for buckled bedsprings with four collapsed beds in a fortnight.

Actually, the hoteliers were not so much complaining about the newlyweds as about the attitude taken by their insurance companies, who had rejected all claims. The question was: had the beds collapsed due to 'accidental damage' (covered by insurance) or due to 'wear and tear' (not covered)?

The insurers were adamant they had the answer, and, you'll be amazed to hear, it meant that they did not have to pay out. Said one dourly: 'If love-making breaks a bed we say it is wear and tear. The same applies to a car engine wrecked by over-revving. It's not covered.'

Several years earlier, a Devon hotelier who had offered cheap honeymoons to newlyweds faced a similar problem. There wasn't a bed in his fourteen-room hotel which had survived the frantic frolics of his guests.

As he surveyed the wreckage, the hapless hotelier said:

'The beds are in such a state - heaven knows what they get up to.

'One bed even collapsed as a couple were using it. One of the legs broke, but they managed to fix it until it could be repaired the next day.'

Finally, the kindly but by now exasperated landlord put up the following cryptic sign in the hope of drawing his plight to the honeymooners' attention:

'Before making love, please consider the landlord.'

It is said that the guardians of the relics of Saint Rosalia in Palermo, Sicily, certainly had cause to regret the honeymoon visit of Dr William Buckland and his new wife to their shrine in 1825.

Buckland was an extraordinary character: Dean of Westminster, a pioneer geologist and palaeontologist, and an enthusiast for all things curious. He would never eat roast beef for dinner when something more exotic was available - tortoise, ostrich and alligator were among the commoner delicacies served up in the Deanery dining-room. Not all Buckland's guests shared his taste for gastronomic experiment, however. One complained wistfully: 'Don't like crocodile for breakfast.'

A visit to view the relics of Saint Rosalia was right up Buckland's street, combining his love of curiosities, his professional interest in religious phenomena and his skill in identifying ancient bones.

Up Monte Pellegrino trekked the Bucklands, to the church of Saint Rosalia built over the spot where the young saint's body had been found encased in a film of lime two hundred years before.

The relics were proudly produced for the great man's perusal. But Buckland was not impressed. 'Those are the bones of a goat, not of a woman!' he cried, and was rather surprised when the local clergy hustled him out of the church and barred the doors.

The marriage of 20-year-old Suad Shaheen to Mohamed Saleh, 29, in Cairo in 1985 turned out to be a disaster for the registrar who had conducted the ceremony.

It happened like this. On her wedding night Suad discovered that her 'bridegroom' was actually a woman. She was really called Bahira Tolba. To add insult to injury, Bahira was already married and had two children.

The police were called. They soon established that Mrs Tolba was in the habit of wearing men's clothes and, that when she did so, she claimed, for some reason, to be a jeweller.

So who got into trouble? Well, not Mrs Tolba/Mr Saleh. Instead, the registrar was carted off to gaol, for the police took the view that he should have seen through the deception and refused to marry the two women in the first place.

Finally, three honeymoon stories which particularly intrigue me.

The first I came across in *Not Many People Know That!* Michael Caine's entertaining book of curious facts. Mr Caine tells us that 'Ethelred the Unready, King of England in the tenth century, was found on his wedding night in bed with both his wife *and* his mother-in-law.'

Now what I want to know is, is being found in bed with your mother-in-law a honeymoon disaster? The answer in this case, I suppose, depended upon what Ethelred's mother-in-law was like, and whether it was his father-in-law who found them.

The second is a most extraordinary story which comes, like so many exotic tales, from the East.

In August 1985, Reuter's man in Delhi reported that a wealthy 61-year-old landowner from Orissa in India had just married his 89th wife. The story went on to say that of Mr Udaynath Dakhinray's previous 88 wives, 57 had either left or divorced him and 26 had died.

Now to have had 89 wives is remarkable enough, but the reason why Mr Dakhinray had embarked upon all these marriages and their attendant divorces and funerals was stranger still. According to the Reuter story:

> Dakhinray pledged himself to polygamy when his first wife left him 36 years ago, just two weeks after their marriage.

The question is, can the first Mrs Dakhinray's speedy departure be categorised as a honeymoon disaster, given that this apparently drove her husband into the arms of a further 88 women?

And here to end this catalogue of connubial calamities is the tale of the poet John Donne and his ill-fated marriage to Anne More. Anne was a niece of Donne's employer, Sir Thomas Egerton, and when her family discovered that the couple had secretly married around Christmas 1600, all hell broke loose. Donne was thrown into prison and lost his job.

Though they were later forgiven and enjoyed sixteen happy years of marriage, the couple were forced to part.

To my mind, Donne's is not only the shortest but also the most poignant of all honeymoon disaster stories. This is what he wrote at the bottom of a despairing letter to his wife:

> 'John Donne, Anne Donne, Un-done.'